DEAR FUTURE LOVER

Bring Your Book Boyfriend to Life

JUDITH JOY

Copyright © 2019 by Judith Joy

All rights reserved. No part of this book may be reproduced or used in any manner without written permission of the copyright owner.

First edition

Editors: Veronica Hughes, Kate Megregian, Sara Lubezny
Cover Design: Dane Low/Ebook Launch/ebooklaunch.com
Interior Design Composition: Rick Soldin/book-comp.com

ISBN 978-1-7335771-0-6 (paperback)
ISBN 978-1-7335771-1-3 (ebook)

Library of Congress Control Number: 2019901064

www.judithjoy.com

This book is dedicated to:

The man I fell in love with, Dr. Bruce Miller.

CONTENTS

1. Introduction. 1
2. A Quick Overview of the Process. 9
3. Levels of Transformation 15
4. Introduction to the Principles. 19
5. Intention. 23
6. Expectations 29
7. Assumption 33
8. Decision Making 37
9. Feeling the Sensations 43
10. Release and Let It Go … Forever 47
11. Willingness 53
12. Wonder and Curiosity 57
13. Questions 61
14. Choice. 65
15. Timing. 69
16. Possibilities 73
17. Rules 77
18. Perspective 81
19. Vibrations 87
20. Vibrational Match 91
21. The High Vibes 95
22. Follow Through. 101
23. Reach for a More Useful Feeling 105
24. Judgment 109
25. Be You. 113
26. Feel the Truth. 119
27. Neutrality 125
28. Signs 129

29	Infinite Beingness.	133
30	Personal Responsibility	139
31	Forgiveness	143
32	Habits	147
33	Perfection	151
34	Create Your Future	153
35	YES!	159
36	Coherence	163
37	Awareness	167
38	Imagine	173
39	Relationship	177
40	Acceptance and Allowance	183
41	Observe	187
42	The Energy You *Be* Is Vital	191
43	Boost Your Vibration	195
44	Feel	197
45	Feed the Feeling	201
46	Silence	205
47	Play and Laugh	209
48	Inspired Action	213
49	Act "As If"	217
50	REM	221
51	Now	223

Appendix

A	Prompts	225
B	Suggested Reading	235
C	Principles	237
	Acknowledgments	241
	About the Author	243

CHAPTER 1

INTRODUCTION

Who Am I?

I am a human being who happens to love learning, and for the past 18 or so years, my learning focus has been on consciousness transformation and energy healing. Consciousness transformation is the process of elevating your attitude, perspective, and feelings within yourself, so you'll be able to reclaim your inner power and start living the life you always wanted. Forget about the traditional ways of using logic-based or known facts and experiences. I've learned that there is so much more possible when we step into the space of infinite possibilities. It's a change that comes from expanding awareness to see the big picture and the multiple possibilities. Energy healing is the same, but it's applied to the physical body. Both are about stepping into a creative reality and expanding the awareness of infinite possibilities.

My journey began with headaches and a quest for a cure. Over 35 years ago, I went the route of regular medical tests but ended up in the alternative arena after Mayo Clinic said, "You have headaches. Take Excedrin." Diamond Headache Clinic said, "Here—have some drugs." And a Catholic hospital in Indiana said, "Put your husband before yourself." That's when I went over to the alternative side.

It started with acupuncture and chiropractic. This was before these modalities were commonly accepted. One chiropractor (whom I still see) sent me to "the guy in the back room." She said, "He taps on your head and you feel better. I don't know exactly how, but it works." It was worth a try. After all, everything I was doing was an experiment on myself. I was open to the possibility that this worked.

And I'm glad I did. This guy tapping on my head was Dr. Ron Jahner, a naturopathic physician, and I worked with him for 18 years—first as a patient, then as a student, and now as a colleague. Along the way, I learned a lot of interesting information that improved my overall life. I'd noticed a common thread between the various self-help theories, energy healing techniques, consciousness transformation programs, and messages from motivational speakers. What I realized was that many of them had the same information, each with a slightly different twist.

So, I asked myself, "What was it about these various bits of information that was causing the changes?" It became apparent that all possibilities are available until we limit ourselves with our conscious and subconscious thoughts and feelings. The more I learned, the more I became fascinated with the possibility of opening up to see even *more* possibilities. I learned that what I think or feel isn't the only possibility. Everything shows up as a possibility and, as a result, no one possibility holds me back. Once I allowed for something to be different...*it could be.*

And as I naturally take the complicated and make it easy to understand, I looked for a way to simplify the information, so I could understand the basics of what was happening across the board. This self-experimentation led me to sharpen my intuition and increase my awareness of possibilities. Then, as I usually do, I simplified the process and began to share it with others through teaching and coaching.

This book shows you how to use these concepts in your life by journaling to attract the dreams, hopes, wishes, and desires you're craving—in this case, your future lover—so you can create the life of your dreams. The simplified process is easy, and you can apply it to your life right now. The hardest thing about the process is to remember to use it. It's really that simple.

What's important about my background?

After my divorce from my first husband, I was a single mom for 11 years. Add to that all the times he traveled internationally, and I was a traveling widow. Now, I've "ordered up" a husband (whom I absolutely love and adore) thanks in part to the letters I wrote to him *before he was even on my radar*. In addition, I'm a mother of four great young adults and two grandchildren so far. I picked up another four children with my second marriage, along with a whole slew of grandchildren and even three great-grandchildren.

My education started with a business degree in marketing/advertising and management/administration from Indiana University, but when I got into the work world, I said, "Maybe not." I'm not really a sit-behind-the-desk type of person. To fill time until I could figure out my next move, I helped to coach the gymnastics team at my former high school, where I'd once been a gymnast. They couldn't pay me since I didn't have a teaching certificate, but I knew my desire was to work with children. This led to my next step...a teaching degree. It was back to school for me, this time to get my Masters of Arts in Teaching from National Teachers' College, now known as National Louis University.

After teaching for a few years, motherhood took over. It was during this time that I began studying energy healing and consciousness transformation as a way to lessen or eliminate my headaches. This time around, my education consisted of following my interests in a more self-directed learning style, which included reading books and articles, going to seminars and workshops from a variety of people who have shifted their lives, and talking with others who knew something that I didn't know but wanted to know. In addition, I worked with private coaches (including Belinda Womack, an angel communicator, and Dr. Ron Jahner, a naturopathic physician and consciousness transformation facilitator) to hone my skills and keep me moving forward.

In all, I was a mother, grandmother, a grade-school teacher, an editor of a business newsletter, a writing coach, a gymnastics coach, a synchronized swimming coach (for a brief blip in time), a dream creation coach, an author, a blogger, and an experiencer of headaches.

Why am I sharing this with you?

Everyone loves to talk with an expert, as if experts are the only ones with the "right" information. But what makes a person an "expert"? They went to the right schools? They have the degrees and certifications someone feels is important? They have written a book…or a few? In reality, we don't need experts. We just need to benefit from others who know that next bit of information needed to move us forward on our own journeys.

Don't take what I say as truth. You shouldn't. Listen to yourself. Test it for yourself. It's just information and a different way of looking at how to get the things you desire. That's it. The information I've learned has led me to have an inspired life—a better life—while being more at ease with myself and others, feeling better, and accomplishing my desires. I call that a win.

I'm so excited that this works that I simply must share it with the world.

Are you willing to give yourself a chance at a better life?

What if you could create a better life than you ever imagined?

What would you be willing to do or be to create a life filled with ease, joy, peace, kindness, and gratitude?

What is my superpower?

Everyone wants a superpower. Everyone has one. A superpower is something that you do so well that you don't recognize its value until you *do*. It's something that people recognize as greater than what most people consider "normal."

My superpower is the ability to take the complicated and make it simple to understand. I can take a lot of information and divide it into edible chunks that I deliver in a down-to-earth way. I build bridges to help your journey move along a little faster. And oh, by the way, the changes can be long-term ones, not just for the next few days.

In addition, I accept people as they are, sense what it will take to get them to their wishes and dreams, and then help them create a pathway to their chosen desires by expanding their awareness of what the possibilities could be by facilitating clarity.

What will you learn?

You'll explore some consciousness principles that will help you have the life you've always dreamed of. You can choose to write to your future lover, or you can use the same method to write to your future children, your future job, your future life, or anything else. Whatever you choose, the possibility is there.

Why name the book *Dear Future Lover?*

To be honest, my love letters helped me find my husband, and my hope is that when you write *your* love letters, you'll attract your future lover, spouse, or anything else you wish to attract.

In effect, what I did was create my own personal book boyfriend. I wrote about him in journal form and then he showed up in real life. Have you ever read a book, loved the hero and then wondered where he is? Your personal journal for *Dear Future Lover* is your chance to create the book boyfriend of your dreams and have him literally walk into your life.

You can create him out of your imagination or you can read books and decide what underlying characteristics you actually like about the characters. For example, are you attracted to a character that is strong, truthful no matter what, comforting and confident? Or are you attracted to a protective provider, who is silent and intense?

Just a hint: Be careful with your word choices. "Truthful no matter what" can also be interpreted as rude. It all depends on how truth is conveyed. And "protective" implies that there is something to be protected from.

The best bet is to choose the feelings you would like to have in your life and realize that the Universe has your back. You will then attract the lover that best fits you.

The more you feel at peace, wonderful about yourself, desirable, and valued, the higher chance that the quality of a person you will attract will also be those things. It all begins with you. What you're feeling…truly feeling on the inside…is what you'll bring to you to experience. If you don't like what comes your way, simply reach for a new feeling within yourself. Let go of what doesn't work for you and accept what does.

It's that simple. My journal worked for me, and I wanted to share what I did so you can attract your desires, dreams, hopes, and wishes. After all, it's my nature to coach.

So, what about the actual letters?

Of course, if I just published my journal, it wouldn't help anyone because there would be no context as to why the letters worked or what the focus might have been. I didn't have this book to guide me—I was just winging it. And it still worked like magic.

That's right. My letters were average letters. Not all of them were spot-on. But guess what? It doesn't matter. This is great news for you. *Just write.* What comes out is perfect. On some days, I wrote a lot. On other days, I wrote a little. What matters is that you share bits and pieces of *you* with your future lover as well as write what you love about him or her. Remember, these are *love letters*. What's important is to infuse each letter with the feelings you will have *when* your lover is in your life. You're preselecting the sensations you'll have so you can start experiencing the sensations every time you write your letters. Start feeling *now!* This may seem like a weird concept, but by the end of the book, you'll be a master at this.

In this book, I've kept the journal entries relatively short by splitting up longer ones. In a few instances, I wrote a new letter as if I'd written it at the time.

Dear Future Lover is organized in a way that helps you learn a principle of consciousness transformation, followed by writing letters to your future lover. You can read the chapters in order, or just open the book and read the one you see.

After the first few introductory chapters, each chapter begins with a principle of consciousness transformation. These principles are why my journal letters worked to attract my future lover to me. By learning these principles, you'll be able to expand your overall life experiences as well as manifest your book boyfriend. You will benefit in every aspect of your life. The principles will help you *be the energy* so you can more easily become and manifest whatever you choose.

Each principle is followed by one of my letters to my (then) future husband. Then, you'll read how my husband showed up in my life in relation to what I wrote in my letter.

At the end of the book, you'll find questions that will aid you in writing your letters to your future lover.

Let's get started.

Chapter 2

A QUICK OVERVIEW OF THE PROCESS

A Letter Written to My College-Aged Son

Dear Adam,

You asked for my advice on how to find a girlfriend. It's really not as hard as you might think. In short, it's about what you're focusing on and what you're choosing. To attract your future lover—or girlfriend, or anything else including a new job, career, or house—you can use a journal to write a series of letters, such as those I wrote to attract your step-dad.

The person (or thing) you're writing to will now be known as Dear Future _____. Fill in the blank with whatever works for you. A lover need not be a spouse, but it's always a plus when a spouse is a lover. Are you hoping to have a lover, a spouse, or just a casual relationship? Decide who or what you're hoping to bring into your life. When you write your journal, use whatever moniker you choose, and if your vision evolves partway through the journal, just change the moniker.

So, how do you start a <u>Dear Future Lover</u> journal? Start with a notebook, lined or not. It's best to keep all the letters in one book so they don't get lost. Now, pick up a pen or pencil and write "Dear Future Lover (or whatever moniker you choose)." You might include a date as you may return to read your journal years later.

You've taken the first two steps! You decided what you desire and have written the first three words. Remember, it's only one step at a time. There will be many more opportunities to expand on your desires. Now, write more.

I imagine your brain is asking, "What am I supposed to write?" This is probably where you get stuck. Try this. Imagine that you're writing a letter to someone who already exists and is your lover, but you just haven't met her yet. Use that imagination. Draw a picture in your mind of what she'll look like, how she'll smell, what she'll feel like, what her values are, and so on. Use all your senses.

Once you have this picture, pay attention to how you'll feel when she's already in your life. Yes, make that assumption. Pull the future into the now.

It's more than a visual—it's the feeling. What's important is how you feel—yes, feel—the actual sensation in your body when you think of having this lover. What feeling are you going for when you and this lover are together? Take time to decide what that is. Once you know the words that describe the feeling, tune into your body and decide what the actual sensation is. This is very important! It's all about the feeling. (Be aware that there may be more than one feeling.)

Every time you write, tune into this feeling. Do as many things as you can to experience this feeling. Writing letters in the journal is only one way. Other things could be paying attention to what you're reading, the words you use, what you're grateful for, and where your mind wanders when you're quiet. There are many ways to experience the feeling, such as dancing, walking in nature, or cuddling up with a pet. Do as many things as you can to feel the feeling. After all, why do you desire the lover in the first place? Because of the feeling you'll have when she's with you.

For example, imagine what it will be like and how you will feel when you have your first kiss. What will your heart be doing? How soft or hard will the kiss be? What will your hands be doing? What will *her* hands be doing? What will you be feeling in your chest or gut?

Once you get into the feeling zone you desire, it's time to write from your heart. Give yourself the permission to feel and dream. No one has to see these letters. This is your own experience with yourself.

When I wrote to my (then) future husband, I pretended I was writing to the man I eventually married. I asked questions just as if I was writing an actual letter. Then, I answered the questions as if he had asked them of me. It was that simple. When I ran out of steam, I signed off. Some days I wrote many pages, and other days just a few paragraphs.

Your *Dear Future Lover* journal will be done over a month or longer. Take time to write each night before bed. Why then? It works at other times, but if you can go to bed feeling the sensation you're hoping to experience, the feeling will stay with you longer. In addition, you'll be setting an intention and, by focusing on it before bed, it will be foremost in your mind as you dream. Both of these will allow the Universe to work for you to find your lover and bring her into your awareness.

But what do you write? Anything and everything that's important to you. One clue: Focus on what you *do* desire. Drop the word "not" from your vocabulary. The Universe works in a funny way. It doesn't see or hear the word "not." And if you write "not," you'll actually become more aware of what you don't desire. For example, "I don't want a giraffe." What are you focusing on? The giraffe. Is that what you desire? No! You get the point.

Most people aren't consciously choosing to have a harder life, always chasing the opportunities but not quite catching them. Yet these same people keep doing the same things over and over, getting the same results. To get something different, you need to do something different.

To have something different, you must remove the roadblocks within you. Yes, within you. Once these roadblocks are removed, watch for opportunities to present themselves and then choose the ones that work for you.

Think of a roadblock as a huge rock in the middle of your path. You're walking along, singing a song and this rock pops up out of nowhere. You keep trying to walk straight on the path, but you continue to bump into the rock. Perhaps you curse the rock. How dare it block your path! Doesn't it see that you, the great king of your life, are walking here? The bumping may go on for years and years. Do you see the absurdity?

Now logically, you'd choose to go around the rock, turn left or right, climb over it, or maybe even pulverize it. The point is that you'd recognize the rock as just a rock. No big deal.

It's the same with emotional roadblocks once you recognize what you're looking at. Then, every emotional roadblock becomes just a rock.

By the way, I knew Bruce was "the one" partly because I'd just told him that "he makes me a better me." Then I reread my journal and found just that phrase—and I'd written it 14 months prior. Fourteen months seems like a long time, but you'll need to let go of the idea that your lover will have to show up exactly as you imagine, when you imagine. Keep in mind that she will show up! Be open to the possibilities in front of you. Measure those possibilities against the feelings and sensations that you decided you'd like to have.

And most importantly, have fun while you write!

Love,
Mom

As a side note: Adam chose to get a dog to fulfill those feelings of cuddling, loyalty, and love he was looking for. He was willing to give up having a real girlfriend for the love his dog provides."

CHAPTER 3

LEVELS OF TRANSFORMATION

Consciousness transformation usually occurs over three levels. Each level is valid and important, but you need not do them in order. You can bounce around, or if you're one of the lucky ones, you can just jump to Level Three and have a fabulous life, where things and experiences come to you with ease, and joy is an everyday occurrence.

- ♥ Level One: Find a problem and fix it.
- ♥ Level Two: Get used to being happy.
- ♥ Level Three: Create your future.

**Level One:
Find a Problem and Fix It**

When everything is working smoothly, there's very little impetus to change, transform, or grow. You're comfortable, so why do anything to change that comfort? You know what it's like where you're at. And what if the change is something worse?

But…what if it's better? What if it's more useful?

Some people are comfortable where they're at and problems aren't a big deal. This is true until it's not. At some point, most people become uncomfortable and have a desire for something to be different. Think of someone, perhaps yourself, who has dated many people. At first, the relationship is great. Then at some point, it isn't. It's at this point—where it's uncomfortable in some way—that this person makes a new choice and ends the relationship.

Or perhaps they don't end the relationship and simply put up with whatever the problem is. They keep doing what they're doing until the problem becomes so big that they can't ignore it, and they are prodded to look for something else. That prod is a problem designed to move them forward.

This is where almost everyone starts their transformation—with a problem. It gets you moving toward something more useful. But beware! This level of transformation is where most people spend most of their time. If you're constantly looking for problems to fix, this means you need problems to be present. And since the Universe will give you what you desire, you'll actually attract *more* problems to fix.

Don't worry. Once you know how to find and fix problems, a funny thing happens. You no longer need problems to move forward and transform. The more you practice these principles, the more ease you'll have in your life.

Level Two:
Get Used To Being Happy
(or whatever high vibe you choose)

We're used to what's familiar and, chances are, you're familiar with whatever energy level you've been living at. For example, think of this as your mood level. Even though you crave a better feeling and strive for it, your physical body interprets this more useful feeling as something *new*. New is different and can be scary, because it's unfamiliar.

What's the big deal? Obviously, the so-called "bad" changes (loss of money, house, relationships, etc.) are stressful, and the body reacts to the change. Here's a secret you may not realize: The same is true of "good" changes, like marriage, birth, or a new job. Each of these changes is something new, and the body must acclimate to the new feelings. Change, good or bad, is still a stress that the body must adjust to.

This explains why, when you feel better and better with more ease, your body just plain freaks out! It thinks it's protecting you from something unfamiliar. This is crazy, right? You feel great, and then your body throws something in the way (such as a headache) to bring you back to how you used to feel. The system (your body) is trying to maintain internal stability and equilibrium…returning to what it knows.

It seems like a never-ending ping-pong game within your body. This better feeling is a new feeling and, like anything that's new, it doesn't automatically feel comfortable and can in fact be *uncomfortable* as your body interprets the new feeling as scary. Your body wants to return to what it knows—the old feelings—and your body will do whatever it takes to keep you safe. This is where you bounce back and forth between the old feelings and the new ones. It takes some focus to get used to the new feeling until it becomes normal.

This is true of any new skill. The more you do it, the better you get. Yes, practice is the key. At Level Two, you're allowing your body to get used to the better feeling.

Level Three:
Create Your Future

This Third Level of Transformation occurs when you create your future without reference to your past. This is where the magic happens! If you had no past, what would you create for your future? There would be nothing to hold you back or sway you one way or another. You'd have total freedom to choose.

Imagine that you never had a bad relationship. Imagine that the book boyfriend you just read about came to life. You could choose whatever you'd like this new relationship to be. You could love freely. You could expect the best and get it. You could have a great sex life without the baggage of past relationships. *You get to choose.*

Once you can recognize the roadblocks and choose to let them go, you're in effect letting go of what's holding you to your past. In fact, you'll be able to imagine your future desire, choose the feeling that you'll have when you have that desire, and then take advantage of opportunities to feed that feeling and focus on the desire.

This is the step where you master your thoughts and feelings. Your thoughts become something to notice and refocus on while your feelings are directed toward the sensations you will have *when* you have your desire. The feelings will literally pull your desires closer and closer to you.

And by the way, this step isn't done from A to Z. Opportunities will come in weird ways. It's up to you to grab them.

So, why is this the last level and not the first? To be honest, the principles you'll learn while going through the first two levels will help support your creations at this level. However, it *is* possible to jump to Level Three and start creating. It's just that most people are motivated to be, have, or do something different because of a problem, and they first desire to get rid of the problem. Then, they need time get used to feeling better to even believe it's possible. But what if you had no issues? What would your life be like? What if it could be better than you ever imagined? This is what Level Three is like.

It's possible! Let's begin.

CHAPTER 4

INTRODUCTION TO THE PRINCIPLES

Principles are the fundamental truths at the foundation of a belief system or behavior. The principles in *Dear Future Lover* will help you create a belief system that supports your life as you desire it to be. Does this mean that you have to change your beliefs? Yes! After all, if you keep doing what you've always done, you'll keep getting what you've always gotten.

But here's the good news: You get to choose what you desire to believe. The principles are guidelines to help you live the life of your dreams. As you become a pathfinder, an inquisitive person, a traveler in your own life, these principles will guide you to find your truth or belief system. It's all about finding what works for you.

I've found these principles to be helpful, and they work for me in my life. This is not an all-inclusive list. The principles for all three levels are the same. The difference is what you focus on. Level One is focused on finding a problem and fixing it; Level Two on feeling better than you could have imagined (and getting used to this new feeling); and Level Three on creating your future as if you had no past.

The principles included are:

1. Intention: Know what you're going for.
2. Expectations: You get what you expect.
3. Assumptions: Assumptions limit possibilities.
4. Decision Making: When you've made the decision, it's "done."
5. Feeling the Sensations: Identify the feeling you're truly after.
6. Release and Let it Go…Forever: Let go to have freedom.
7. Willingness: Willingness is the magic pill of change.
8. Wonder and Curiosity: The gateway to magic is in the sense of mystery.
9. Questions: The wiggle room is in the question.
10. Choice: The choice is yours.
11. Timing: It will show up when it shows up.
12. Possibilities: Keep reaching for a more useful possibility.
13. Rules: Beliefs we tell ourselves are true for us.
14. Perspective: Perspective determines reality.
15. Vibrations: Highest vibe wins.
16. Vibrational Match: Whatever you're feeling is what you're attracting.
17. High Vibes: Ease is found at love, peace, and gratitude.
18. Follow Through: Take the next tiny step.
19. Reach for a More Useful Feeling: Things can be even better.
20. Judgment: Let go of fixed points of view…including judgments.
21. Be You: Quit compromising against yourself.
22. Feel the Truth: It's only true until it's not.

23. Neutrality: The art of being at peace.
24. Signs: Pay attention to the signs around you.
25. Infinite Beingness: Expand and be all of you.
26. Personal Responsibility: It's your life. Take responsibility for it.
27. Forgiveness: Forgive yourself and others.
28. Habits: Create new habits.
29. Perfection: What shows up is perfect…on some level.
30. Create Your Future: You create your life.
31. YES!: Take charge of your life. Say YES!
32. Coherence: Flow with the river.
33. Awareness: There is nothing you need to be or do to be who you are.
34. Imagine: All of life is made up. Imagine your future.
35. Relationship: Balance the relationship to neutrality.
36. Acceptance and Allowance: "Should-bust" your way to a higher vibration.
37. Observe: Zip it, watch, and listen.
38. The Energy You *Be* is Vital: Be to become.
39. Boost Your Vibration: Be the true you.
40. Feel: What feeling are you truly going for?
41. Feed the Feeling: Feel the sensations you will have *when* you have your future.
42. Silence: Take time to listen.
43. Play and Laugh: Play is the creative energy.
44. Inspired Action: Prepare for the arrival of your desires.
45. Act "As If": Pretend you already have your lover.
46. REM: Repetition. Emotion. Motion.
47. Now: The only time is this moment.

The first four principles are important, but not for the reasons you may think. People talk about intentions, expectations, assumptions, and decision making as if they are the end-all-be-all. In reality, they are beneficial...sometimes. However, they can be limitations that hold you back from your true desires by constricting the outcome. They are preconceived notions that are locked down.

The clue is to introduce "wiggle room" into each one and allow for more potentials and possibilities to show up. Recognize that where you start doesn't have to be where you end up. Ask yourself, "Is it possible to be, have, or do (something) without limiting myself to what I can see or know now?" After all, you can only see or know what you see or know.

However, if all the possibilities are available, then there is at least *one* possibility (and usually many more) that's different from what you are already aware of. Leave a little wiggle room for your intentions, expectations, assumptions, and decision making to grow and change as you progress. Can you allow for something better than you can imagine?

CHAPTER 5

INTENTION

Know What You're Going For

What are you looking for?

Why were you drawn to this book?

What do you hope will be different in your life?

I'm serious—when you picked up this book, what were you hoping would happen? Whatever that is, that's your intention.

But even before you made that choice, did you determine how you're going to show up before your future lover does? That's right—you get to choose. You get to decide whether you're going to show up as a shrew or as a loving and kind being, filled with peace and love. The choice is yours.

From that choice, the Universe will bring you experiences to coincide with your intentions. The first step is to decide how you choose to show up. Then, when the Universe brings you experiences, you get to decide if they'll help you fulfill how you choose to be. Once you decide how you intend to be and show up in your life—in every encounter—you can move to the next question: "What do you hope to attract?"

Since this book is titled *Dear Future Lover*, chances are pretty good that you're looking for a new love in your life. This is probably a new interpersonal relationship such as a husband, wife, girlfriend, boyfriend, partner, lover, or someone that fits in another category but will still be in a relationship with you. For simplicity, the book is written from my point of view (since its basis is the actual journal of love letters I wrote to attract my husband). It includes examples for creating a new relationship. In my case, the desire was masculine. Use any gender you wish. Remember, the methods in this book can also be used to create a new job, buy a house, improve your business, or any other thing.

Once you know what you're looking for, ask yourself to look a little deeper. Are there any underlying intentions that you hadn't considered, and now would be nice to acknowledge? For example, one underlying intention is that by writing to your future lover, you will be able to attract him into your life with ease. This can seem obvious; after all, you picked up a book about writing a journal to attract your future lover. It's slightly different than just hoping for a new relationship. The difference? It's more than just reading a book. You're agreeing to write a journal of love letters to your future lover.

And as for the ease? Why not set the intention that the whole process (including him showing up) is done with ease? After all, it doesn't make much sense to hope that it's difficult. But if you choose to, that's up to you!

Think of underlying intentions as setting up your parameters. If you're looking for a husband and you have no other requirements, *anyone* will do…even that creep down the street.

Take some time. You'll be able to come up with a few more details. But don't worry, as the whole process is designed around ease. If you can think of the parameters now, great. If you think of the details as you are writing your journal entries, great. Whatever works for you.

These underlying intentions can be very specific (blond hair, blue eyes) or they can be more general (what you'll feel when you're with him). Personally, I prefer the general, since I went for the feeling I wanted to have and didn't limit myself to a specific outcome. I was open to allowing the feeling to show up in a more useful way than I could have imagined.

Take a moment and think of the book boyfriends you are attracted to. What do they have in common? What is it that you truly would like? If your book boyfriend showed up at your front door, what would you find truly important about him?

Be Purposeful

Setting an intention is being purposeful. Everything we do has a purpose, even if we aren't consciously aware of that purpose. This allows you to get rid of the clutter in your mind, and as things are clearer, they become easier. When we know what we truly desire to accomplish, our focus brings us into the moment, the task is easier, and other possibilities to achieve the purpose come into our awareness.

The first time I wrote out my intentions, I thought my future husband had to come from a certain religious background. But eventually, I let go of this limitation in my thinking (intentions are limitations by design), and opened up to the possibility of a partner from a different faith. And that's exactly what I got. We're very accepting of each other's idiosyncrasies, including our different outlooks on religion.

When you know what you truly desire, the Universe will move mountains to help you achieve those intentions. Additional possibilities will pop into your consciousness and, very often, they'll be even more useful ways of achieving the true intention you're striving for. The Universe is on your team, so put it to work for you. Let it know what you truly intend, and then set it free to find it.

Think of the Universe as a restaurant. If you give the waiter your order, he knows what to bring you. However, if you are ambivalent, he doesn't know what to suggest or what to bring you. A clear, concise order (intention including your sensations when you have the intention) makes it easier for the waiter (the Universe) to give you what you truly desire.

Then, let go and allow the Universe to bring you great opportunities!

Are you ready to begin? Let's get to the first letter. I'll present my letter as I wrote it in my journal. (I've taken the liberty of mixing up the order to better fit with the order of the principles.)

How you write your letters is up to you. Don't be concerned about every part of it being perfect. There are two ways (and probably more) to write these letters. You can just write whatever comes up (as I did) or do a bit of planning and decide what your intentions are for each letter before you write.

Dear Future Lover,

I don't know if we've met yet, but I imagine this has not happened. Otherwise, I'd feel some pull toward you, some instant spark of attraction. You know the kind—the one where our eyes search out each other's across a crowded room. Maybe we've been introduced...maybe not. Either way, it would be an invisible thread of energy drawing us together and neither of us is able to (or wants to) escape the web of silken desire.

This all sounds like a fanciful way to say we instantly like each other, but already I know that my life with you will be more—more fulfilling, more enhancing, more alive. You'll help me to be more me. To come into myself. Hopefully, I'll help you to also be a better you, not that there is anything wrong with you, but only the best version of you. I guess I'm trying to say that we will bring out the best in each other.

What part of you do you feel is still hidden? As you'll soon find out, I'm full of lots of questions. Sometimes, they can seem intrusive. But I ask because I'm really curious. I don't ask something of you that I wouldn't ask of myself. But then, I'm used to asking myself the hard questions and then searching for the truth in, behind, or under what the first answer seems to be.

Some of this is who I was, and some of it is who I've learned to be. Either way, I like this search for truth. It certainly is more interesting than the mundane stuff most people talk about—the sound of the train passing, the color of xyz, the value of one belief over another, or politics.

That last one is a boring category all its own. As you can see, I'm not really into politics. It seems that I never have the whole story. There is always some information slanted or even missing. So, decisions aren't based on truth, only versions of it. I was in advertising and public relations long enough to realize that these versions of truth sometimes aren't anywhere near the truth. It's funny, but I never put together this disconnect between politics and truth as the source of my discontent. I learn something new every day.

But before I go to bed, I'd like to try to answer the question I posed. What part of me do I feel is still hidden? The answer on the surface is—the real me. I've lived my life trying to please others. In the process, I forgot or perhaps don't really know how to please me. Whether it's sex or what to eat for dinner, I'm more inclined to put myself aside and try to please the other person. This works for a while, but I always end up mad. It's almost as if the pleasing phase hooks the person, then when I try to please me, the other person feels confused and betrayed, not understanding the shift.

> Sometimes, I don't understand it either. It comes at me like a freight train—faint whispers in the distance, rumbles as it approaches, power as it blasts through or by, and then wind as it (and the relationship) is carried away.
>
> It's gotten to the point that I don't even try, but then pleasing is so ingrained in my persona that I easily slip into it.
>
> Please help me be a better me by being true to myself—and to you at the same time.
>
> Good night, my love. Sweet dreams.
>
> J

So, what actually happened? How did this letter influence the outcome?

After a few months of writing, I put away the journal during some cleaning frenzy and forgot about it. Fourteen months later, after I met my husband, I happened to come across it. What struck me was that I'd just told him that "he made me a better me." And he continues to do so. He is very encouraging and supportive of my desires. For example, he was willing to fill in the gaps in our daily living as I wrote this book. As my focus was on the writing, he often did things like grocery shopping and cooking so I could continue writing. He was willing to go without my company and attention as the words were jumping onto the pages.

CHAPTER 6

EXPECTATIONS

You Get What You Expect

Now that you've set your intentions, what are you expecting? You see, you'll get just what you expect. It's more than what you say you desire. Your expectations are all the various rules you've made up about your intention being a certain way, combined with your feelings about them. Very often, our expectations don't match up with reality, but we can't see what's truly happening because we expect something else.

Think of an expectation as the intentions beneath your initial intention. What are you expecting by having a relationship? What are you expecting the relationship to be like? What are you expecting will happen when you are in *the* relationship?

These are a few questions to ask yourself to clarify your actual expectations. Often, we're unaware of our real expectations, or we just make assumptions. Your mind says, "Of course, I'll be happy when I meet my future lover." However, on the inside, you're freaking out and feeling something along the lines of, "Happy? Are you nuts? Every relationship I've ever had has led to drama and trauma. I'm tired of it!"

In fictional books, the characters have some level of drama or trauma to make the book interesting. These are the expectations we have when we read a book. In real life, we often aren't running from terrorists, being kidnapped or getting stranded on a desert island and all the feelings these evoke. Thank goodness!

Pay attention to what you are expecting in real life. If you're saying one thing (I'll be happy) but feeling another (drama/trauma), you aren't congruent. Your thoughts and feelings aren't in agreement. And here's the kicker...*what you feel rules the roost*. Your feelings are what you're actually attracting.

Later in *Dear Future Lover*, you'll learn to neutralize the feelings and have more coherence. For now, just recognize that you may have some expectations that are different from your desires—just notice them for now.

There's one more important point about expectations. If you expect something to show up in a certain way or at a certain time, you're limiting the possibilities. It's more useful to keep yourself open for something even better and ask, "What else is possible?" This works especially well when you can keep your expectations to feelings you desire instead of specific outcomes.

Dear Future Lover,

I was so proud of Adam yesterday. The Sunday began as many others had—lazy, with friends after a sleepover. I had a headache, so I withdrew...first TV, then reading, then a hot bath.

By evening, as I was getting ready for a bath (to raise my body temperature), Adam and I started looking at the essential oils by the tub. He picked up Deep Relaxation and told me to put it on my temples. I also put it on the back of my neck where it was tight. Then I took Bufferin and magnesium before getting into the tub. By the time I got out, my neck was very relaxed, and the headache was gone.

In addition, Adam let me know that the handle for the powder room door was broken, and his phone was being held hostage.

We spent quite a long time taking apart the lock, with a little phone help from a friend.

So why am I proud of Adam? Earlier in the evening, I'd asked him to stop watching TV and do something with me, and Adam pointed out that we were doing something together—not what we had intended, but we were still doing something together. Being able to see how an intention can be filled in many unexpected ways is a wonderful skill. Yay, Adam!

And now I'm proud of an internal discovery I made. I was doing an exercise to fully describe a time when I was happy. I chose Bethany's wedding. As I thought about it, I asked myself, "What was different about this time?" Well, that was the perfect question. Yes, I was happy about Bethany being happy, but the big difference was that I was doing what I wanted, not what others expected of me. For example, I sat at the table with my friends instead of with family where I would have taken care of my dad, who wasn't feeling great. He had Goldie, my second mother, for that. I danced as much as I wanted. I asked for what I wanted, for example, another glass of champagne when mine was cleared away before I'd finished it. It was great being the mother of the bride.

The big difference was that it never occurred to me to please others. That's not true. But at least when it did, I dismissed it and did what I wanted—instead of sitting on the sidelines afraid to do anything for fear I wouldn't please someone. And it was fun.

It looks like I'm on the way to fun. Yay for me. I wonder when I'll be able to take the leap to the new energy. Not that I'm rushing, but I'm finally feeling good about it.

More later,

J

So, what actually happened?
How did this letter influence the outcome?

When my husband and I planned our wedding, the feeling we were after was *fun*. This was the measuring stick as to whether we included something in the wedding or the reception. And the comment we received over and over after the wedding was that it was "so much fun." We realized that the marriage was what was important. The rest was just a party. And the party was fun. By setting the intention as fun, we were also expecting everything to be fun. So, when something didn't match our expectations, we could change it or let it go.

CHAPTER 7

ASSUMPTION

Assumptions Limit Possibilities

An assumption is defined as taking something for granted or accepting it as true or certain to happen without proof. Most people look at an assumption as something bad.

I had the assumption that my oldest, Bethany, was behaving because she was quiet and well mannered. However, she did way more than I'd imagined while in high school. And since my kids have graduated from high school and the "statute of limitations" for punishments has run out, I'm finding out more and more about what went on that I had no idea about.

Here is one example from when she was still in high school. It wasn't until she almost graduated that she happened to mention, after reading an article in the paper about a party being busted, that she was supposed to be at that party. Lucky for her (no punishment) she was home with a sore back. I'd never realized she was a partier. Today, she is a wife and mom with two kids, and between work and family, partying is reserved for an occasional night out.

And since then, I've learned to look at what I assume to be true and question the validity of it. This is very useful, because we are often mistaken based on other things that have happened or are happening. It's more useful to look at what is actually happening, not what we assume is happening.

Assumptions often show up as phrases so imbedded in our culture that we just assume they're true. Think of the saying, "All the good ones are married." Or "I can never find a man like that." What you have just told the Universe is that these men don't exist for you. The Universe gives you what you desire, so it says, "Okay. They don't exist for you."

These phrases aren't actually true unless you make them so. It just derails your imagination and limits the possibilities. By making statements such as these, you haven't given the Universe any wiggle room to create. You have just stated what you think reality is…not what reality can be for you.

What if we're just looking at it backwards? Why not have the principle of assumption work in your favor? Start imagining *what you desire*. Instead of imagining all the bad things that might take place, start imagining what you'd like to see and put your energy *there*. Assume you already have it. What you focus on is what you get.

Here's the kicker…*assume it is already here*. This shifts the energy from worry or seeing it in the future (which actually means you're experiencing the lack of it, and your focus is on the lack) to gratitude for having it, which is a much higher vibration. (Refer to Chapter 19 for more on vibrations). Thus, what you imagine will have an easier time finding you.

Dear Future Lover,

When I started writing tonight, I had the intention to write about a book I just started reading—How to Be Single. This is a funny choice for a book, especially since I've been writing to you, my future husband.

Anyway, the thoughts I wanted to bring up (after only 90 pages of reading) are about beliefs. The first is that "There is no reason to buy into the belief system that there are no good men left." I felt like this was a Gibbs head slap. Duh! (Adam says if I'm quoting from NCIS, I'm watching too much of it.) This statement opened my eyes and let me see that I never even questioned the idea that there are no good men left. Obviously, there are. After all, I found (or will find) you. But for sure, the "good men" will be somehow elusive if I hold that belief.

The next head slap is about love—"It will happen. It always does. Why worry about finding it?" Combine that with "How can love ever find you if you don't believe in it?"

I always knew that I believed in love. However, I tend to think that part of me is pushing it away, expecting or assuming it will hurt. This is definitely something in my releasing future. As soon as I can let it go, I know you'll be there. Hey, maybe you already are, and I'm just not seeing the connection.

I look forward to meeting you.

Love,

J

So, what actually happened?
How did this letter influence the outcome?

I'm so used to clearing assumptions that I'm always shocked when Bruce makes what is so obviously an assumption. When I'm nice about it, he is more than willing to look at clearing his assumptions. As a result, he is finding it easier to be more accepting.

CHAPTER 8

DECISION MAKING

When You've Made the Decision, It's "Done"

You've picked up *Dear Future Lover* and read to this point. You took an action step toward your desire for a "lover."

This is the hardest step, and you've already done it! You made a decision. It's just a possibility until you have chosen. The act of choosing is what makes something a decision.

We all have the ability to make a decision. We determine what we do with that ability. For some people, this is difficult; for others, it's easy. But in the end, *you make a decision*. However, remember that when you *avoid* making a decision, you are, in fact, making one!

What can help you decide more easily?

Take time to determine how you choose to be—before the moment arrives. You have the ability to create the moment instead of just reacting to what shows up. Think of it this way—if you know what you desire to be (for example, loving and peaceful), then when someone comes into your awareness, you will know if they can help you to be that or not.

The same is true of your desire for a future lover. Once you've decided what you choose to be, you can decide what you'd like from your future romantic relationship or from the individual. The relationship and the individual are different. They are not the same, even if one influences the other.

Knowing what you decided ahead of time (rather than just reacting to what shows up) will help guide you so each decision can be supportive and lead you on the path to accomplishing what you set out to do. However, if you never decide what you truly desire, *anything* will be good enough. (Remember the creep down the street from Chapter 5? Do you hope to date him? Can you imagine spending every evening with him? Can you imagine him being a contribution to your life or you to his?)

If you don't decide what you really desire, then anyone is fair game, and anyone is good enough. And every time life presents you with an opportunity (say you meet someone), you'll have to decide if he's right for you. However, if you've pre-chosen the parameters, you're more likely to know if he's "the one" and if he helps you to be more of what you choose to be.

You're looking for someone to fulfill you in some way. That special person will make you feel a certain way. It's this feeling that you're after.

When I got divorced, I already knew that I was going to be married again someday. That decision was made. While I was waiting for this choice to materialize, I decided to clear up my own feelings and did a lot of inner work so I'd be the best me when I did attract my future husband. And if I never did, then at least I'd be happier with me.

After all, my first relationship is with myself. This is where I made the decision to be expansive love…no matter if I was in a relationship or not. I don't always hit this goal. Quite frankly, I forget sometimes that it's my desire to be expansive love, but then something happens to remind me.

When a situation pops up, we all run on habit patterns. We react to what happens based on how we habitually acted in the past. It's what we know. To move past this, ask yourself this question: "If I choose to be _____ (fill in the blank with your feeling choice), how might I show up in this situation?" (Note: Any of the letter prompts at the end of the book can also be used to bring forth a new you. Just change the focus to "Dear Future Me.")

Once I decided what I chose to be, the next step was to determine the qualities that my future lover would have. I wrote a list of qualities I desired in a future spouse. I actually listed about five or six pages of single-spaced writing! I preferred a man who rolled up his sleeves, was kind, and was faithful... among many other things.

Once I felt comfortable with the list, I set it aside and started dating men that I met through friends and on dating websites. It was interesting how simply observing these men allowed me to think about what was on my list and how it all played out. It kept me from jumping in to fulfill a momentary need. I focused on the real desire...being expansive love *and* marrying the man of my dreams. Don't give up the future goal for an immediate desire.

As I went on dates, I refined the list. For example, I went on a date with man who was very nice. But he cut out magazine articles for me, loved peanut M&Ms, and preferred chunky peanut butter. These are qualities my father has, and I recognized them as such. I went back to the list to see how I'd set this as a goal. It turns out that I'd written, "a good father figure." I'd meant for my *kids*, not for me. I revised the list.

Another man I dated drank more alcohol than I did. A lot more. It hadn't occurred to me to put anything about this on my list, so I added, "sober." I figured that sober would also include staying away from drugs—something else I'm not interested in. And it was a positive way to say I didn't want someone who was drunk and did drugs.

After a while, I realized that there were too many things on the list. So, I started playing with my list. Were there general categories that would fit into a few major groupings? What feelings would these general categories represent?

It was amazing, but I was able to reorganize the list into something much simpler. I ended up with the feelings I was truly hoping to attract. These feelings could be from my future husband or from other areas of my life. I was looking for communication, connection, laughter, play, enthusiasm, love, and peace.

Dear Future Lover,

My mind races with ideas wanting to get out, yet my pen lags behind with the thoughts that were much like my life—an afterthought. How sad to only now realize how my life has been a hesitation until I'm behind, even before I began.

I guess, in a weird way, this has shown up with my hairstyles. My hair is finally long (which by the way took two years to grow, and the latest styles are short.) Long hair makes my face appear long and sad. When I reflect on my high school senior portrait, I remember the same. I remember that day. I'd been sick, and the paleness of china alabaster skin reflected in the portrait was further made somber by my long hair dragging down my smile, which never quite made an appearance. Fear of the future? Boredom of the moment? Energy drained from preparing, primping, dressing, and then driving to Rogers Studio on Devon and Sheridan? The exhaustion was preserved for prosperity in the picture everyone would someday see. Of course, this was during my Green Phase, the time when many of my clothes were green and yellow, further dragging down my visible energy. Where was seasonal color analysis? Not yet invented. Winter—that's what I am. Winter. I do well with jewel tones, especially the ones with red and blue. Just recently, I've expanded into melon and orange.

But I digress. How unusual. Ha, ha, ha.

Sometimes it feels as if my mind is a pinball machine randomly lighting up as the trajectory of the stainless-steel ball changes once it hits upon something. Here, even in my acknowledgment of my digression, I digress. The only thing to do is laugh at the absurdity of it!

I've strayed from hair. One day in my freshman year of college, depressed because I was depressed (do teens really need a reason?), I was walking on Third Street in Bloomington, Indiana, when the idea popped into my head to cut my hair. It was fall. How appropriate that my hair should fall also.

Of course, passing the beauty shop (or was it called a salon already?) prompted the idea. But the significant thing is that I acted on it. I didn't think it over, agonize about what to do, or ask anyone what they thought. I just acted.

I remember going into the shop, asking if anyone was available, then calmly saying to the stylist, "Do anything you want." Oh, if only I could live my life like this—open to the possibilities, not afraid of the outcome. I'm getting there, but not quite yet.

By the time I left, my hair, which had reached to my bra hooks, was on the floor. This was before the days of donating hair for wigs—or at least I think it was.

I continued my day and my life with a new trajectory. My short hair—above my ears—freed me from whatever had been weighing me down.

And yet, here I am thirty-five years later contemplating the same thing. The difference is that I hesitate, search for opinions, and then ultimately do nothing. I don't even like long hair on me. My shoulders rise up to hold the tips behind them so that it doesn't fall in my face. Very often, my hair is only in a ponytail, which I love to swing, but in reality, this is only another version of short and off-the-face. When I look back on pictures, I see that I was perky with short hair. I miss those days. Fast, easy, ready to jump into the day. Who am I kidding? That was never me. What a sad thought.

Yes, my life is happening all around me. Sometimes, I forget to jump on the ride. That's where you come in. I know that when we bring out the best in each other, we'll be on the ride of our lives.

Love,

J

So, what actually happened?
How did this letter influence the outcome?

As it turns out, Bruce's mind is more of a pinball machine than mine. He's an inventor and is constantly looking for new ways to do stuff. So far, he has three medical patents. Check out www.burnsolutionfoundation.com for more about one of them.

And as for my hair, I've since cut it, and he loves it. (I recently saw a picture of me with long hair from then. Yuck. Where were my friends? Certainly not advising me.)

CHAPTER 9

FEELING THE SENSATIONS

Identify the Feeling You're Truly After

What we truly seek is a feeling. We do things because they will give us feelings. Most people are in search of things that feel desirable. In the letter below, the emotion is actually the excitement of writing down ideas. The feeling (also known as a sensation) was the buzz within my body and mind which felt very uplifting to me. While the letter didn't focus on what I'm looking for in my future husband, it did focus on a big part of my life that I chose to share. After all, if he's going to marry me, then this bit of information is important for him to know. By writing it down, I'm in effect sending it through the cosmic air waves to him.

Often, we aren't consciously aware of what we truly desire—the real feeling we're going after. Once we identify that, we can allow the Universe to bring it to us in many possible ways.

You see, all of our feelings have energy attached to them. It's usually this energy that charges the experience and directs us to take specific actions that lead to various results. This works if we're getting our desires. Very often, however, what we're getting isn't exactly what we're hoping for. Thus, if we can neutralize the charge and change the energy, then the actions we choose will most likely be different, and thus the result will be different. (You'll learn more about neutralizing the charge in Chapter 27.)

Most people start with a thought that leads to an instant feeling about that thought. From there, they take an action and then evaluate whether the action gave them the result they thought they wanted. If so, they keep doing it. If not, they go back to the thought and try to change it.

With *Dear Future Lover* letters, you start with a desire and then choose the feelings you'd like to experience. From there, you take inspired actions, one of which is to write to your future lover.

If the feelings show up in other ways, great. This way you get to experience the feelings in more ways than just through your one desire. You aren't relying solely on your future relationship to supply that sensation. For example, you're thinking about what you hope to say, infusing it with love, and then writing the letter. In the process, you're feeling the loving sensation, and the Universe will bring other experiences to you that match that sensation.

Let's take a moment to consider the sensation of love. If you already know what it feels like, then all you have to do is feel the sensation before you begin to write. The feeling will come through your words.

If, however, you don't know what love feels like, think of something such as snuggling a baby or a favorite pet. Imagine the warmth within your chest as you cuddle with it. Imagine looking into its eyes as you smile and it returns your smile with one of its own. Imagine the baby smells. (Not the dirty diapers!) Imagine the sigh of contentment you're feeling. Imagine every aspect of your experience. Feel the sensation in your chest as it fills with love.

Feeling the actual sensations, you will have *when* you have your dreams, desires, hopes, and wishes is where the power is. The feelings have energy—vibrations—and these vibrations will bring your dreams to life.

Dear Future Lover,

Sleep is elusive tonight. The writing fairies have decided that tonight is the night to download ideas. My mind is so busy that every time I close my eyes, another idea bubbles to the surface, and I can't relax until I turn on the light and record it. It almost feels that if I don't write while the ideas flow, then I'll never write. What if this is a one-time idea and tomorrow the feeling to write dries up?

Just the thought is enough to stop the writing.

If I hadn't told Adam that I'd drive him to school tomorrow morning, I wouldn't worry about staying up until the ideas were all written down. But I did promise to drive him, and I do want to rest.

My intention is to sleep well and awake feeling refreshed. However, the conviction is a bit thin, as it's already after one in the morning.

Sleep well my love,

J

So, what actually happened?
How did this letter influence the outcome?

There is an element of excitement underlying this letter. While this isn't the love mentioned in the above section, excitement and enthusiasm are two of the sensations I was looking for in a relationship. And Bruce has certainly introduced those.

Never in a million years could I have imagined myself going to sprint car races. I didn't have anything against them—they just weren't in my awareness. I'd never been exposed to them. That is, until I met Bruce. He once raced sprint cars, and he still loves to watch them. He's even exposed my kids to something that I never would have done on my own. He's taken them from joking about the "excitement" of turning left (over and over) to actually enjoying the sport. Sprint car races are a lot more fun than I'd imagined! And watching them has given me many opportunities to practice my energy healing during the crashes.

A bit about the crashes. The first time Bruce told me about sprint cars, he sent me a video of crashes and told me about the time he hit the wall at 130 miles per hour. My first response was, "You're nuts!" I didn't see the excitement of crashing and possibly killing yourself every time you got on the track. I've since learned that there are many safety mechanisms in place.

However, we struck a deal. For every car race he takes me to, I get to take him to a ballet or another dance show. We're both expanding our horizons.

CHAPTER 10

RELEASE AND LET IT GO ... FOREVER

Let Go to Have Freedom

Now that you know you're tuning in to the sensations in your body, the next step is to be able to release them. I can hear you now—"What? I just found them! Now you want me to let them go?"

Think of it as freeing yourself from their energetic push or pull. For if you "have to have" or "can never have," the feeling is influencing you. What is truly happening is that *you have a feeling about the feeling*. Let's call this underlying feeling X. Just as X marks the spot, this X (the underlying feeling) is what your experiences will gravitate toward. For example, if you are focusing on love, but the underlying feeling has more to do with how your last partner cheated on you and you can't trust love, then this "not trusting" feeling will infiltrate your feelings of love and screw things up for you.

It's best to get to the point where you're okay if it happens or if it doesn't happen. After all, wouldn't you rather know that no matter what, you'll be all right if you are in the relationship or not. Getting bent out of shape isn't very useful. Being able to let go of what you're sensing or feeling about your future lover actually opens the energetic space to allow love to show up more easily.

And by the way, when you aren't holding onto the underlying feeling, you feel lighter, as well as more expansive and freer.

Your old underlying feelings (the ones you haven't let go of yet) have implanted themselves within you and are refusing to let go. They are literally fighting for their lives.

Think about it. If the old feeling thinks it's keeping you safe, then it's doing its job…stopping you from repeating the "so called" mistake by reminding you what it feels like. It's saying, "Oh no! Watch out! If you do that, you'll be hurt. So, I'm here to save the day. I'm going to remind you what you feel like when you're in a relationship. You can't do those anymore. I'm not leaving you. I'm your hero!"

Unfortunately, it's doing the opposite—bringing you experiences to prove "it" right, which are not the experiences you really desire.

Yuck.

You are your hero. *You* get to decide what you feel like.

Whether your feelings are hanging around "to protect you" or you've absorbed them from something else, you can make a different decision.

Clearing the emotional charge attached to your thoughts can give you room to choose the feelings you desire. There are three simple ways to clear the charges. Choose the method that works best for you…auditory, visual, or kinesthetic.

Why are these important? The only thing that makes one style more valuable than another is to decide which one works best for you. If you learn by hearing information, you're auditory. If you learn by seeing information (in pictures or words), you're visual. And if you like to learn by doing an activity and physically moving, you're kinesthetic. You may be a combination of these. There is no right or wrong; use what works best for you.

You may ask, "What does this matter for reeling in my future lover?" (Notice the word "reeling"? My husband is a fisherman, and I reeled him in with my journal.)

The first step is to recognize that you have a sensation in your body. Your chest constricts. Your stomach feels like a million butterflies are inside. Your throat closes up, and so on.

Your body is talking to you. What are you going to do with this information? You get to make a choice. Are you willing to allow the possibility that this sensation can be released?

I've divided the releasing methods into learning styles so you can recognize those that may work for you. And if you don't get results with one, try another. Remember…whatever works. Let's get started.

Auditory

Hear it. This involves someone talking and you listening. Or it could be you listening to yourself as you talk. (Again, whatever works.) This is where questions come into play. Ask the Universe for what you desire in the form of a question, such as, "What will it take for my future lover to appear in my life with ease?"

Listen for the answer, feel the sensations in your body, and then ask yourself, "Whatever that feeling is, am I willing to release and let it go forever?" It's your choice. If you ask and are willing, the energy will clear. You may have to ask a few times for all the energy to clear.

We'll talk more about questions in Chapter 13.

Visual

See it. This is something you can see in picture or word form. Make a picture (in your mind or on paper) of what you would like to happen—your desire. When you do this, your body will feel a sensation.

Imagine opening windows in your body to let the sensation leave. You can even wash the "rooms" in your body to remove any remnants of the sensation. Check in the closets and under the furniture for any lingering sensations!

Notice that at some point, the visual morphed from just "my body" to "my body as a house." Pictures morph. They are living, breathing images that can change. This is beneficial. This is uncovering information.

This next step is important. *Fill the space with love.* Feel what this feels like. Here's a clue: Anything other than love is a lie. Love is our true nature.

Kinesthetic

Do it. Move. Act it out. This can be an extension of the visual style. For example, pantomime and pretend you chop up the sensation, grab it, and throw it out. Then fill the space with love as you use a fire hose to pump in rose-colored light, representing love.

It's said that "thoughts create things" and "thoughts create reality." This isn't exactly right. It's actually the emotional attachments that are attached to the thoughts that pull your "reality" to you. And here's the great part—you get to choose the feelings…if you can let go of how you used to feel, and if you're willing to be neutral. (You will learn more about neutralizing the charge in Chapter 27.)

Dear Future Lover,

Complaining. What are your thoughts?

Personally, a little bit is OK. However, continuous complaining is boring—even my own.

You may ask, "Why this subject?" Well, I was reading a book tonight. Don't ask why it took me an hour to put it down. It *just did. Anyway, it seems as if all the characters in the book were complaining. Dreadful to the max. I really need to get to the bookstore. Am I willing to let go of this book and have something better? You bet!*

What are you reaching for that feels better?

J

As you can see from the short letter and even the sign-off (no love, smiles, chuckles, or any other endearment), my own feelings were dragged down from something that happened on the outside...reading a dreadful book. I literally absorbed the yucky feelings and lost the wonder and excitement of writing to my future husband. The *outside* feelings became *inside* feelings. I hadn't been feeding the feelings of my desire.

So, what actually happened?
How did this letter influence the outcome?

The first year we were dating, I took Bruce to five different energy or consciousness programs and teachers. Each one did a form of "creating your future through releasing old feelings." He hadn't done this before, but he was willing to try just because I did it. At the end of the year, I asked him which he liked the best. We then stuck with that method.

Truth be told, I was already blending them together. What I eventually learned was that if I could *be* the feeling of love and share that energy, the other person could choose to accept or not accept the love vibrations. From this vibration of love, miracles happened. That's what it all boiled down to. Bruce actually got the benefit of that as I shared the love vibration and shifted things within his body, consciousness, and experiences.

Chapter 11

WILLINGNESS

Willingness Is the Magic Pill of Change

Everyone is looking for the magic pill, some easy method that will just shift things and deliver desired results. Willingness is it—the magic pill. It's the key to creating the life you desire... including the future lover you're currently writing to.

Willingness usually implies a cheerful readiness to do something, but it's so much more than that. It also includes consenting or giving permission.

Think of it as cheerfully being ready to do something. How does this apply to creating your future lover? It's asking yourself, "Am I willing to _____?" That's it.

You're giving yourself permission to have what you desire and let go of what no longer works for you (including all those funky underlying sensations mucking up your desires). Make the choice. Give yourself the power. Choose willingness over and over.

Are you willing to let go of whatever you're holding on to?

If you are reluctant to let it go, you might as well grow it and experience more and more of that sensation. Looked at this way, it seems pretty silly to hold on to anything.

Here's a hint. If you're willing to let it go forever, then you're also consenting to let something else *replace* it. This is true of whether the sensations feel good or not. This principle is especially useful when you realize that you can pair it with a rule such as, "All changes work in my favor."

By asking the question, you're freeing yourself to let go of the old and allow for the new. It's in choosing willingness that you open the space for change to occur. The clue is to step into the feeling of consenting and saying "yes" to something being different.

By the way, are you willing to release and let go forever whatever sensations appeared when you read, "All changes work in my favor"? I'm sure you felt something.

Dear Future Lover,

It's amazing how we construct our lives to accomplish our goals without questioning if the goals are still valid or, in fact, ever were.

What are your goals? Have you ever looked at your unconscious goals, possibly even the ones implanted by your parents, teachers, or even society? There are so many rules we live by and goals we strive for that don't have anything to do with us if we actually took the time to examine them. Once you go down this road, all bets are off. We really can construct the life we desire.

While I know this, I sometimes forget. Just the other day, I was saying something about waiting until I get married again to redo the TV cabinet in my bedroom, so you (my future husband) will have some say and maybe even overlook the red walls I love so much. I'm trying to please you already, and you're not even here!

But then a friend said, "What if he likes what you like?" Amazingly, I'd never even thought of this as a possibility. Duh! Sometimes, our way of thinking is so ingrained that we don't even see it.

Am I willing to let go of everywhere I think I know the outcome and allow a better outcome than I could even imagine? You bet.

Am I willing to release and let go forever whatever is holding my limited thoughts in place? YES!

Shoshi just walked in, so I'll go for now.

Smiles and chuckles,

J

So, what actually happened?
How did this letter influence the outcome?

Red is his favorite color, and he loves the walls. By the way, I painted them red, because I wanted passion in my future relationship. For me, red represented that.

CHAPTER 12

WONDER AND CURIOSITY

The Gateway to Magic Is in the Sense of Mystery

They say, "Curiosity killed the cat." Whoever *they* are is still up for discussion, but the point is that this phrase is now part of our everyday language. More importantly, if you align and agree with it, it's limiting you from being curious. It is literally programming you to not be curious. After all, if you're curious, you may be killed like the cat. What limits you is your belief that there is truth in the point of view.

However, when you can stay curious and open with wonder, you're letting go of preconceived notions that hold you in place. The magic is in the wonder because the very act of wondering opens the door of possibilities.

While you're writing your letters, the more you can stay in the feeling of wonder and curiosity, the more magic you'll be able to create. And from this magic your future lover will form and come to you.

Notice in the following letter that I left open possibilities and asked questions that may or may not be answered. I let go of the idea that things had to show up *in a certain way*. This gives the Universe the opportunity to bring me something more useful than I imagined.

Dear Future Lover,

The more I write to you, the more real you are becoming. I guess that's part of the purpose of these letters. I wonder how you're going to show up in my life? Will you walk up to my front door and introduce yourself? Will we meet at a seminar or class? Are we going to simply run into each other? Will someone introduce us?

There are so many options. It's sort of exciting—like knowing that a gift is coming, and not knowing when, how, or what it is.

Of course, I know what a husband is, but I don't know the details. How will we fit together to make a more complete whole? Don't get me wrong. I'm not trying to figure it out—a major no-no in releasing. I'm just wondering.

Wondering is so much fun. It opens all the windows of possibilities. Have you ever tried wondering how things will show up and then let go, waiting for the movie to begin?

We go to a movie with the intention of being entertained, and then we sit back to watch. We don't try to control what happens on the screen. And even when we try to influence the movie with a well-placed "no" or groan, it doesn't work. Obviously.

Today, I was releasing on receiving and feeling worthy. I kept flipping the energy* of what showed up and then letting it go. I wonder how this will show up in my life.

Of course, it started showing up right away. I opened a magazine and read an article about a man who thought he was in the right place, but it just didn't feel right. He sat under his thinking tree, quietly waiting. An idea popped into his head—start a new church instead of trying to change one.

The message for me is to start new instead of trying to change something.

So now, I ask the Universe, "What?" I guess writing these letters is a new way to bring us together. Trying to fit in and change wasn't really working for me. Computer dating sites aren't founded in truth. That's not really where I want to be.

I wonder how else all of this will show up throughout the day, week, month, and beyond?

I wonder about you. Excitement is beginning to flutter in my chest. It's time to let it go as I sit in the warm morning sun overlooking the bluff, staring at the lake beyond.

Anticipating you,

J

---

*"Flipping the energy" is a term I use when I'm playing with energy. Think of it as an energy coin with two sides. The first side is what is felt now. The flip side is a feeling that is more useful. Flip the energy coin until the more useful feeling is on top. That then becomes the "now" feeling. Flip the energy coin again. Physically flip an invisible coin. You will know when to stop when you feel an expansion and deep breath.

So, what actually happened?
How did this letter influence the outcome?

As it turned out, a friend *did* bring us together at a seminar while on a cruise. And yes, Bruce *did* walk up to our table and introduced himself. I guess I was aware on some level what would happen. The wonderment left open the possibility for something even better…I had no clue that a cruise would be involved.

And as for the continuing wonder, Bruce is an inventor, so it's there also. He even tolerates all my wondering questions.

CHAPTER 13

QUESTIONS

The Wiggle Room Is in the Question

Questions create movement, whereas conclusions and judgments block and create stagnation. Movement is important because if you already knew the answer (for example, who your future lover will be and how you'll meet him), you'd already have the solution. But since you're reading this book, chances are you haven't met "the one" yet.

Since you're moving toward a new relationship, questions will help you get there. They will help you define what you desire in the relationship and what you'd like it to look or feel like. They will help you navigate the process without causing you to be stuck as a conclusion or judgment would.

Be sure to ask questions that move you forward instead of trying to figure out the past. This is important. You already know where you've been.

Chances are you're probably comfortable in finding a problem (looking backward), asking questions, and fixing it. Those questions are known as *reflective* questions. While these are sometimes effective, too often we keep asking about the past, reflecting on what was, thus keeping the past alive. The result is often that we focus on the problems and wonder why we aren't creating a different future. Remember Level One of

Transformation? If you look for problems, problems must keep popping up…and very often this is what the reflective questions are about.

The real challenge is to look forward and ask questions that will help you get there, all the while knowing that you're living in the now and what you ask *now* will help direct your *future* (Level Three of Transformation). The ideal is to ask questions to help you create the future you desire and help you follow what works for you to achieve that future.

There are two types of questions, and both are valuable. Open-ended questions (the essay type) dig deep and uncover possibilities and things you didn't know you were thinking until you asked the question. They stir things up. The second type are closed questions (yes/no) which provide a choice, but no new information.

Here's how they can work together. Begin with an open-ended question: *What is the greatest contribution I can bring to this future relationship?*

Do you see how asking this type of question opens the possibilities for new information to pop up in your awareness? This is the basis for the open-ended questions.

Now, for the closed questions. We use these when we'd like to make a choice; for example, when we're letting go of any stuck energy that appears as a sensation in the body.

Read the question again: *What is the greatest contribution I can bring to this future relationship?*

Notice your body right now. Do you feel something? It could be an initial inhale, a cough, a tightening in your stomach or chest, or any other sensation. Whenever you notice the sensation, ask yourself, "*Whatever that sensation is about* (and you don't have to know what that is), *am I willing to release and let it go forever?*" This is the closed question.

At this point, you don't have to do anything other than choose to be willing to let it go.

With this type of releasing question, you can choose one of many words to free the hold that the emotion has on you… *destroy, uncreate, release, let go, neutralize, harmonize, dissipate, dissolve, drop, pop,* or another. Each word has a slightly different meaning, and thus has a different power within you. Choose the words that work for you.

Now, for the *Dear Future Lover* journal, ask yourself open-ended questions. It's most useful if your questions begin with "what." Don't worry about the how or why. Feel what comes up. Then ask a closed question—ask if you're willing to let go of that sensation, and then write about it. You can ask your future lover questions you're interested in, and then answer them as if he'd asked you the same questions.

Dear Future Lover,

What's taking you so long? I'm patient, but I'm really missing your touch. Love can be conveyed through a casual touch, but real love—the kind felt in each beat of the heart—only comes about when a touch melts into more and becomes the soup of our lives.

Here I am trying to be romantic and I come up with soup! Well, at least we will always laugh.

But the idea of a blended family as soup is pretty good. We get to decide how we would like the flavor of our soup to turn out. Are you the chicken? Maybe. I'm the jalapeno. Whatever we are, we'll be together.

Do you think I'm waiting to meet you until this journal is done? We really can meet before the final page. I can finish it after I meet you.

Tad says that he sees me meeting you in a tiki hut. He says you're tall, thin, and have white hair. That's okay with me.

I found a penny on the ground. Yahoo! That seems small, but it's still something different. But the big change is with the ravine restoration project. Two years ago, it was estimated to cost mega bucks. The bids are much lower—drum roll please—6.66% of the estimate. That's the total cost, not the savings. It was an accumulation of things—the recession, the park district wanting to build a fishing habitat in the ravine, and the contractor wanting a show piece as well as business. Add to that the fact that I was neutral about the entire project. This allowed all the good to flow to me.

What flows in your life? What experiences have you had that created even more flow? If life was truly flowing for you, what would that be like?

Talking about good flowing, Adam is on a winning streak in wrestling. His record so far is 7–1. It's 10–1 if we include demonstration and exhibition matches. He really is doing well. Something clicked for him this year.

Time for bed. Sweet dreams, my love.

J

So, what actually happened?
How did this letter influence the outcome?

My husband *does* have white hair—but then, he's 14 years older than I am. And as for the tiki hut? We met on the lido deck of a cruise ship. Does that count?

CHAPTER 14

CHOICE

The Choice Is Yours

Every day, many things happen that you interact with. Someone yells at you, or you get cut off in traffic. You watch a pharmaceutical commercial play on the TV. You walk past a makeup counter in a department store and think of someone special. Your alarm goes off late (or quite possibly you failed to set it). The thing is, how you react is up to you. You have a choice. It doesn't have to be an automatic response.

This is where releasing and letting go fits in. To be truly free to make a choice, you have to be free of whatever is holding the emotion in place. The freedom from the emotional push/pull will give you the space to more easily make a choice instead of just reacting.

When you pay attention to your feelings (and how your body feels) you'll know when it's time to switch to something different. If you're getting antsy and can't sit still, make a different choice. If you're slumped down and can't breathe, make a different choice. If you keep looking out the window and are easily distracted, make a different choice. If you are about to walk into a tree, make a different choice.

What most people don't realize is that you get to change your mind…a lot. In fact, you get to make a choice, evaluate it, and then make another one if you so choose. You do this all the time. That cute guy you met last week would be good to date. You date him and then decide he may be *cute*, but he's not worth dating, so you look for another choice.

Life happens moment by moment. The past has already happened. The future has yet to happen. And still each of those is made up of moments. In reality, we only have this moment to make a choice. Then it is done, and we are on to the next.

We may as well live each moment as it happens and let go of the ones that have already happened since they are no more. It's just memories of the moments that we hold onto in the neurons in our brains.

If your brain is filled with the past, you repeat the past because that is where your focus is, and what you focus on is what you get. If you are thinking about the future, you might worry about what may or may not happen, and your focus is on the moments that haven't even happened yet. Therefore, depending on how you see those moments and where you are focusing, you are influencing your future.

After all, a choice only lasts a moment. In the next moment, you can evaluate if your choice worked for you? If so, keep doing it. If not, make a new choice. When you make a choice, *it's only a choice*. You can change your mind. But if it feels expansive within your body to make the choice, your body will thank you for following through.

Dear Future Lover,

There has to be a more useful term I can use than "future lover." Nicknames seem phony, and they aren't my style. Of course, if I knew your name that would solve the problem. But, alas, I don't.

It's always possible to call you "Honey" or "Dear," but "Dear Honey" sounds like I'm writing to a woman. "Dear" just sounds strange. Well, if it's like other things in my life, the solution will pop up in the near future. Who knows? You may too!

I wonder what you look like. All day, I've tried to zone in on your looks. The only thing I can see at this time are your eyes. They are as comforting as melted chocolate. I sigh just thinking of it.

When I look elsewhere in my vision, I hope for broad shoulders, strong with muscles and character. I imagine myself lying in your arms protected by the mass framed within your shoulders and strong arms. Let's not forget chest, as long as I'm drooling.

But that's really it so far. The vision is a bit sparse, but I know it will develop over time.

Dreaming,

J

So, what actually happened?
How did this letter influence the outcome?

We have a great energetic connection. As for making choices, we're both open to new ones. As it turned out, this whole nickname deal is something my husband wants, but I still can't find a suitable name for him. My subconscious picked up on the problem long before my conscious mind did.

And as for the broad shoulders and strong arms? Yes, my husband came equipped with those also. And I love playing with the hair on his chest we lie together, and I listen to his heart beat.

CHAPTER 15

TIMING

It Will Show up When It Shows up

Your desires will show up when they show up, so let go of your attachment to the idea that things must occur within a certain timeframe. Everything happens in its own time. Stay open to the possibilities.

Your job is to align yourself with the feelings and sensations of your desires. The more in alignment you are, the less confusion there will be about what you're asking for, and the sooner it can show up. All you have to do is get excited about it, and it will move forward.

What are your assumptions about the timing of receiving? That it will take a long time for your future lover to show up? That he can show up instantly? That you have to go through trials and tribulations before you can have your future lover? Do you have to search for him, or will he come to you? Something else?

While you're waiting for your future lover, ask yourself, "Am I willing to let go of whatever is in the way of my future lover appearing?" Pay attention to the feelings and thoughts that pop up. It's the willingness to let them go that will allow the wiggle room for something to be different.

The more neutral you are about everything, the sooner something can show up. The idea is that you're not holding on to or resisting anything. If you're neutral, your desire can come to you.

If you have conflict in your desires, whatever has the strongest feeling will win. For example, if you desire a future lover, but covet your alone time to the point of obsessing about it, guess what you may have more of? Alone time. This doesn't bode well for having a companion.

Release and let go of feelings, thoughts, words, and actions that may be holding you back. Look at things from a new perspective that could include *both* of your desires. Then expand your feelings, looking forward to what your life will be like when you have your true desires. You may go down the road of, "Oh no—this will cause that. And that will cause something even worse!" But you don't have to do this. In fact, that's actually pushing you further and further from your desire.

Remember the timing? Even if you're totally in alignment, it may still take time. The other person may have to finish something before he's available for you. Trust and know—have faith—that he's coming. Your future lover has been especially picked out for you, and a few things may have to line up before that can happen.

Dear Future Lover,

I planned on finishing yesterday's letter this morning, but just didn't, which turns out for the best. Tonight, I felt like watching a movie, so I chose "Sleepless in Seattle." It wasn't until I was done that I realized it was something else with letters and romance.

What's the deal here? Maybe when I get done writing all these letters, you'll appear. Sounds good, but why limit the timeframe? It could be faster.

Love,

J

A side note: This letter is not in the order in which the letters were written. Other letters previous to this one, talked about writing letters popping into my awareness.

So, what actually happened?
How did this letter influence the outcome?

As it turns out, my husband lived 1,200 miles away when we met. We needed to wait until we were in the same location in order to meet. And after we met, he moved to *me* while my youngest son finished high school.

As soon as we'd started dating, I had a feeling that if we stayed together, we'd spend a lot of time in Florida (where he's from). So, I started covertly looking for a town that I liked in Florida. Most of the towns weren't what I was comfortable with, but just before we got engaged, we drove through one that I loved. It had the vibe I liked. Thus, I had the town picked out before ever really needing it. After we got married, three of my kids moved home for various reasons, so my husband and I went to Florida for the winter…and I already had the general location chosen. Using energy, it took only three days to find "the place."

And as for the letters, while we didn't actually write letters, we made a lot of phone calls. And in the seven and a half years since we met, we haven't missed a single day of talking.

CHAPTER 16

POSSIBILITIES

Keep Reaching for a More Useful Possibility

Even though you don't know who your future lover is, are you willing to allow the possibility that he can be even better than you could ever imagine?

Each possibility is a potential. If all the possibilities exist (and they do), then certainly there is at least one (and probably many more) possibilities that are more useful than you can imagine. So, are you open to receiving them? Are you willing to get out of your own way?

According to quantum physics, every possibility exists until you have chosen one, and then all the other possibilities fall away. Think of it in this way—you're looking for a future lover. If all the possibilities exist, then this includes everyone of both sexes and all ages and possibly even aliens. (Ha ha!)

What? That's not what you want? Okay. Fine-tune the possibilities by sex, age, location, race, religion, and so on. Your pool of possibilities has now become much smaller, and it will continue to do so until you have chosen "the one." That doesn't mean the other possibilities have disappeared. It only means that you aren't seeing them as potentials.

This is a great place to look at the possibilities you love about your book boyfriends. You may be reading about

28-year-old heroes, and yet you would never imagine that at 40, 50 or 60 you would be interested in someone so young. Or maybe you are. That's okay too. Whatever works. The point is to consciously choose the possibilities you would like to become a reality for you.

Or you can look at a broader spectrum of possibilities, you may find love in many different places and from many different people. The "lover" you are looking for may or may not be one of them, but at least you'll have more love in your life, because it will come from many different directions.

When you increase your possibilities by focusing on your true desire (the sensations you're truly going for), you open yourself to find something even more useful. This is when the possibilities presented feel more expansive and more closely match how you choose to be.

Keep reaching for a more useful possibility…even if you don't know what that possibility is. In this way, you'll be able to open to more and more possibilities.

How I used this in my life is illustrated in the following letter, when I told my future husband about my son (who was 14 at the time) hurting his neck during wrestling practice, and how I kept following the possibilities until he felt better.

Dear Future Lover,

Annette is convinced that the energy I do is powerful. For example, take Adam's accident yesterday.

First, Adam's astrology yesterday was set up for major disaster. It's only set up this way once every two years, apparently. I don't know much about astrology, but I'm open to the possibility that there's something there.

Whether the astrology foresaw disaster or a darker journey, Adam's body and communication all balanced out because of my clear intention and attention. You see, Adam hurt his neck at wrestling. He lost energy, his hands tingled and his shoulder hurt when he tried to put on his sweatshirt. I called the chiropractor, who said he wasn't even to pick up a pencil. We went to the ER for a CT scan and x-rays for possible concussion and a broken neck.

But as I told Adam on the way there, "We aren't in the morphic field of a broken neck yet." I set up the field that everything would be fine, and then kept flipping the energy. I felt major shifts happen. I even felt a tingling in my fingers when I "felt" C4 without touching it. As it turned out, the diagnosis was a bulging disc between C3 and C4 (vertebrae in the middle of the neck).

When we got to the ER, I calmly said we were there for a possible concussion and possible neck fracture. Everyone jumped, as I knew they would. We were helped immediately, and they put him in a neck brace.

As we waited for the x-rays, I could feel Adam's anxiety increase. I'd been laid back and everyone there was very careful, but the anxiety increased. I gave Adam direct orders. "I know that you're feeling anxiety, but I want you to let it go! I don't care how. You can have fireworks come out of your chest, but you will let it go." I kept on flipping the energy.

After a time, the energy shifted. Jahner says at the beginning all the nerves in the neck were firing and active. Three hours later, only one spot was "hot." I continued to play in the energy off and on all night. At about 7 a.m., I had my hand on Adam's neck while doing energy and I felt a bubbling in the spine. I knew that the energy around the bulge shifted.

As it worked out, my massage therapist was coming this morning, not his usual day, so I had him massage Adam.

Then we all decided the chiropractor was the next to work on Adam. Everything went back together easily.

Annette says it was my clear intention and attention on the energy that made the difference. This was a sign to me of how powerful energy really is.

It could have gone down the road of a darker journey if I hadn't been so clear that everything would be all right.

When I mentioned this astrology to Adam, he pointed out that it was almost exactly two years ago that he'd hurt his fingers. But I think it was his foot. The fingers were in February. Adam sees the possibility of how astrology has an influence in our lives.

So, in conclusion, you'd better watch out. As I flip the energy around sex, it will get clearer and stronger. I'm really beginning to look forward to our great love/sex life.

Love,

J

So, what actually happened? How did this letter influence the outcome?

My husband has experienced me playing in the energy field with him numerous times for various different things from health to business to, of course, sex. Three times, I've called an ambulance for him (medical help is certainly a possibility to be open to). However, I kept feeling for more useful possible outcomes and was able to find them. Let's hope there are no more ambulances in his future. But wait—we *do* want one to show up if he needs it. So, let's rephrase that. Let's hope for continued great health.

Chapter 17

RULES

Beliefs We Tell Ourselves Are True for Us

Unfortunately, many of us think that what we feel is "right" because that's what we're used to feeling.

There is a story about a baby elephant with a rope tied around its ankle, with the other end of the rope attached to a post. The elephant couldn't move very far because the rope and post were stronger than he was. As he grew, he accepted that he couldn't move more than a few steps because what he felt was his reality. By the time the elephant became an adult, he could have pulled the whole thing out and walked away. But he'd given up and just accepted that the rope was stronger than he was. He did nothing, and stayed exactly where the rope was.

Along the way, we've managed to pick up false beliefs, just as this elephant did. They may have worked for us at one time, or maybe we unconsciously accepted a belief and agreed to it. But the important thing is to realize that many of the beliefs we live by aren't true for us. They can be true for someone else, but we can choose better beliefs. ("Better" just means they work *for* us instead of *against* us.)

The same is true of the rules we live by. The rules that we made up to support the beliefs (which were a result of our perceptions) may no longer work for us. It's okay to make up new rules that work in your favor. The level of emotions surrounding the experience, the number of times the experience was repeated, and the physical action that accompanied the experience help determine how strong the belief is and possibly even what the belief is.

These beliefs are the rules we choose to live by. However, rules can lie. Lies cause the body to tense, the blood pressure to rise, and a general feeling of unease to take over. This tension is a disagreement between the conscious mind and the subconscious mind, and it shows up as a reaction in our bodies. Unfortunately, this physical reaction very often shows up as physical ailments and diseases. It becomes stuck, because the belief is stuck.

Imagine going through life afraid to have sex. As children, many parents teach their kids that sex is wrong. Gradually, these children find themselves in a relationship (possibly a marriage) where sex is normal, but they hold on to the old rule that it's wrong. How is that working for them?

Here's the thing. You get to choose the rules you live by. You make a choice instead of following a rule just because it's there. A rule is just a statement that you or someone else decided was "right." But if you have total choice, you might choose the same thing from a totally different energy.

Take the idea of having an affair. There are lots of rules about how this is wrong, such as, you can't have an affair because someone told you not to.

But what if it was a choice? (In truth, if there is no judgment, then every possibility is actually a choice.) Now, imagine looking at it as a choice. Imagine you're presented with an opportunity to have an affair, but you choose not to. You say, "I love my spouse and would never desire to hurt him/her. Thank you for the opportunity, but I'm choosing my spouse."

In the end, you choose not to have the affair, but the energetic feelings about how you got there are different. Allow the rules to work for you on all levels. Choose the rules that work for you. Make choices based on the energetic vibrations you choose.

Dear Future Lover,

OMG! I've just had the most amazing session with Annette. She's helping me uncover the rules I live my life by that I don't see. Annette and I seem to speak the same language. But what is the topic, you ask? Sex, of course!

JT said to me this week that he felt when I kicked him out of the house, it contributed to his feeling that he can't rely on women to be there for him. I apologized for my part in this belief that he was holding on to, but said, "Let's look below that." By the time we were done (only about five minutes) we got to the belief that he didn't feel worthy. We then looked at how this could play out in his life—injuries (not worthy of winning), people leaving, things not going his way, etc.

This was fascinating. This was the first time he let me dig this deep. I looked at the situation when I kicked him out. (He'd been disrespectful by doing things that I'd asked him not to. Shoshi was also asked to leave at a different time when she couldn't restrain from the same things.)

Annette helped me see what's under the issue from my point of view. I had a belief like, "How dare they have fun in my house (when I'm not)!" Substitute body for house. Then work down the chain to the old victim morphic field of a woman not having control of her body. I can choose the new morphic field about having control of my body.

> As we talked, I was flipping the energy. The new rule is still sticky, but I'll keep refining it until it feels like it will work for me. Annette and I are convinced that, once this is a neutral subject, the magic will happen and the gates of love will open.
>
> Loving you even more,
>
> J

So, what actually happened?
How did this letter influence the outcome?

I've become more neutral with my feelings about sex and intimacy (yes, this was a part of it). My husband was always comfortable with it and has been very patient as we have grown closer and closer.

CHAPTER 18

PERSPECTIVE

Perspective Determines Reality

People see their beliefs as reality. However, this "reality" is only one option. Yes, that's right—reality is based on your perception, which is based on your perspective. Someone else who is having the same experience may have a different "reality."

Here's another elephant story. Three blind men are trying to determine what an elephant looks like by touching one part of the animal. The man touching the elephant's leg says it's like a tree trunk. The one touching the tail says an elephant must be small, like a rope. And the man touching the side of the elephant "sees" it as a huge wall. Each man experiences his own reality based upon his perspective.

You can see that they're buying into their limited viewpoints, because they think that what they feel is all of it. And in the same way, we tend to believe our limitations just because we don't know what else is possible. Our limitations restrict or define our perspective. Thus, they form our reality.

When you have one point of view and your future lover has a different one, both of you are operating from limitations. For example, let's say your point of view on opening doors is that you don't need him to open doors for you, and you get insulted if he thinks you aren't capable. His point of view is that he was taught to open doors for women and views it as a sign of respect. If you each hold onto your point of view, one person will "win" and one will "lose" as he either does or doesn't open the door. In reality, you *both* lose because you will both feel the agitation, which isn't exactly love.

Ask yourself some questions:

- ♥ Are you willing to accept that each of you has a different viewpoint?
- ♥ Are you willing to back off of your point of view long enough to say (nicely), "That's an interesting way of looking at it"?
- ♥ Are you willing to let go of any judgment about something being right or wrong, good or bad? (Just by asking these three questions, can you feel some of the tension lessen?)
- ♥ Are you willing to be open to a new possibility that works for you more than you ever imagined?
- ♥ Are you willing to allow that something else is possible?
- ♥ What am I not understanding that if I looked at this from a different viewpoint I would understand?

As you can see, the less importance you put on either point of view, the less you have an attachment or resistance to it turning out a certain way. This is important because if you're attaching or resisting then you're restricting the available choices.

Once you let go of your attachment or resistance to that point of view as the "right" one, you can begin talking about a more useful solution. Your goal is to be open to the possibility that both of you can be happy with the outcome and feel even more loved.

After talking about it, you may realize that when he opens the door, he's showing you (and the world) that he values, treasures, and loves you. He may see your need (by the way, a need is a limitation) to be independent. Together you decide that every time he opens a door for you, he's saying, "I love you." From this perspective, both of you feel loved. In addition, he knows that independence is important to you and supports this in other ways. Whatever you decide, you'll have let go of needing to keep your point of view, and this leads to more possibilities.

Dear Future Lover,

Adam was watching the movie *The Invention of Lying* when we started talking about lying. The pros and cons. How being polite is sometimes lying. And, of course, about people taking advantage of others by lying.

At this point, I asked Adam if he had to stop lying (even little white lies), where would it show up in his life? Then I wondered where it would show up in my life. I'm not a liar by habit, but I'm certainly a product of advertising, public relations, and of course, trying to please others.

But when I thought about it—for all of a second or two—I surprised myself with my answer. I'd quit saying "I'm fine"* when I'm not. This seems like a major step for me. Then I began to wonder if I was saying "I'm fine" because no one is really interested, because I really am fine, because I'm trying to convince myself I'm fine, because I don't want to increase the negative energy, and so on.

Then there are times, especially when parenting, that I say something is fine, but on the inside, I'm cringing, knowing that what came out of my mouth doesn't match my head or heart—both of which then begin to hurt. Why do I hurt myself so another person isn't disappointed? That's pretty stupid.

> Well, tonight I did say exactly how I felt—and I was respected for it. It felt like a breath of fresh air to be clear in my head, heart, and mouth. It's interesting how these opportunities pop up.
>
> So now, I'll ask you...if you had to give up lying altogether, where would it show up?
>
> By the way, it's interesting to note that, when I was a kid, my dad would tell me, "You don't have to be quite so honest." My dad is very honest, so it probably was about being harshly honest. Although I find I like it when I am. Life is easier.
>
> Truthfully yours,
>
> J

*In the years since writing this letter, I've changed my mind... sort of. I still won't lie, however, I will choose to find something that is terrific and then say, "I'm terrific." It's not necessary for me to try to fit into what others are expecting. In fact, I like shocking people. No one actually expects me to say, "I'm terrific." And that gives me a chuckle, which helps me feel even more terrific.

So, what actually happened?
How did this letter influence the outcome?

As it turns out, my husband also doesn't lie. Yeah!

And as for the door-opening bit, I usually get my own car door, but I let him open other doors for me (when I remember). We did agree that when we are dressed up and go out, I'd like the "full treatment." It just feels special.

My husband has been learning how to tap into his true desires and to express what they are. While reading a romance novel, I ran across a very nice explanation of why a man wanted to open doors for his girlfriend. I read it to Bruce, and he said, "Yeah. That." We laughed at how well the fictional character was able to express his feelings and how hard it was for Bruce to verbalize his own feelings.

CHAPTER 19

VIBRATIONS

Highest Vibe Wins

This is the "secret sauce" of consciousness transformation, energy healing, and super-turbo-charging your desires. The highest vibe wins.

This is how it works. Energy is the force that allows everything to happen. It's measured in vibrations and felt through feelings or sensations.

The Universe works through vibration, and everything vibrates—people, animals, plants, food, clothing, colors, pictures, words, thoughts, feelings...everything! Every molecule vibrates, even if we can't see it. The vibration sends out a signal to everything else in the Universe. This signal (vibration) looks for other signals that are the same to "hang out with" and attracts those things to the original signal. This is called *attraction*.

Thus, if you would like more ease and joy in your life, then raise your vibration until you are actually feeling ease and joy, which will then magnetize experiences that match this high vibe. *Be to become.* You need to be the feeling (for example, ease and joy) before you can become whatever has those feelings (the experiences).

The higher you vibrate, the more energy you will experience, and thus it will take less actual action to do things. When you're feeling apathy, grief, or depression, you probably don't have a lot of get-up-and-go. It's hard to help yourself, let alone others. You don't have a lot of energy to get things done. This is described as "feeling down."

As your vibe rises, you have more energy, and everything gets easier to do. Move up the scale to anger, and you have the energy to be angry. Your anger pushes you to create change, unless you like being a victim and choose to remain one.

Now, move further up the scale to love, joy, gratitude, calm, peace, and kindness. These are the times when you feel great, and what used to seem difficult now happens with ease. It takes almost no effort to get stuff done. This is described as "feeling up."

Just find what feels good for you. Then find what feels *better* and then what feels even better than that. The better you feel, the higher your vibration goes, and the easier it is to manifest what you actually desire in your life.

Obviously, if you want to create change, raise your vibration to take advantage of using less effort. and you'll find the change happening with more ease. Be the energy you wish to be or attract.

I said that the "highest vibe wins." What is this about?

A person who is angry has more energy than someone who is depressed. In this case, the highest vibration is the angry person. But introduce someone with a *higher* vibration, say someone who is filled with gratitude, and you'll find that this person will actually use *less* energy and be able to create change more easily. It can be as simple as putting a thought into the room and watching as the thought pops up. The person with the highest vibe "wins," and their vibration has the greatest effect.

I do this all the time. I was once in a meeting, and I was tired. My part was finished, and I wanted the meeting to end. As the highest vibe in the room, I energetically put the thought

"I'm done" in the room, and then sat back to watch. The speaker stopped talking, looked perplexed, and then said, "I'm done. I think we've covered everything."

Believe me, I was just as shocked as you when this worked! Yes, "highest vibe wins" does work.

Dear Future Lover,

Yesterday, Dr. Jahner and I played in the energy with my accepting or receiving love and affection. We played with my relationship with Shoshi, dating, my power, etc., and then let it all go.

Next, we briefly touched on, "Am I tired just for me?" Then, "Am I eating just for me?" As weird as this sounds, it worked. I shifted the energy and realized my exhaustion wasn't all mine. After clearing the perception, I wasn't tired any more. (I'd been falling asleep in meetings, or at least trying not to.)

Then the food idea of eating for myself was interesting. I'd made a big dinner with a lot of interesting tastes but only had one helping. I didn't want any more. Jahner reminded me that we'd played with food, eating, and weight. Oh yeah. I just wasn't as hungry.

Shifting from my perception to the reality of my higher self is a very powerful tool. I'll bet you're wondering about the accepting love part. Frankly, I am too. It will be fun to see how this shows up in my life.

As a healer, I'm comfortable with giving love. When Jahner and I started playing, I couldn't even imagine receiving it. Silly isn't it? But last night, I had a dream about being married to a complete nerd whom I loved deeply. We had three girls—maybe 11, 9, and 6 (or younger). I wonder what that means. Surely it wasn't literal.

> When I woke up, I imagined you in bed with me. As you started kissing my neck, I smiled and giggled, relishing the feeling. I really giggled out loud. A moan or two even escaped. This is cool stuff.
>
> I'm looking forward to when it's real.
>
> Sending love,
>
> J

So, what actually happened?
How did this letter influence the outcome?

Bruce is very comfortable with sharing love…as long as everything he thinks he has to do first is done. However, I *have* been known (at least in my own mind) to rearrange his priorities. And when I do, a funny thing happens. The more I know what I desire and then put it into the Universe, the easier it is for me to be comfortable, and it just shows up.

Thus, our sex life is improving. For example, once Bruce came home from a week of visiting his father—his best friend. As soon as he walked in, I said, "I just read a 'sexy' part of the book and you'll reap the benefits." After an enthusiastic hug, he went to unpack his suitcase, shower, shave, and so on. I was fuming. So, since my energy was highest, I rejected him and we never had fun that night.

Another night, the same thing almost happened, but I'd learned my lesson. I put into the Universe the idea that we would make love. And then I proceeded to feel as if we would. I kept the space open for something even better. And we had much more of an emotional (and physical) connection.

CHAPTER 20

VIBRATIONAL MATCH

Whatever You're Feeling Is What You're Attracting

When vibrations match, they come together. Feelings that vibrate together stay together. We tend to get in a rut with our feelings and experience the same ones over and over. It's almost as if we have a set point and don't venture too far from it. But it doesn't have to be this way.

You can choose to have a different feeling. You can change your vibration and feel more expansive, which will lead you to attracting a higher-vibrational partner.

Think of the people you've dated and all your book boyfriends. They usually have something in common. They feel comfortable in some way. They feel familiar. Their vibration matches yours. This is often why, when people get divorced, they end up dating someone very similar to the person they just left. (Remember: It doesn't have to be this way.)

This is true even if intellectually you're looking for something more favorable. Until *you change your vibration,* nothing changes. The choice is yours to feel anger or gratitude. When I was getting divorced, I wrote lists of gratitude for my soon-to-be ex and for the "mistress." I was determined to have a higher vibe. It wasn't until I got to "she took him off my hands" that I could truly feel the gratitude. And am I glad I did! She's a wonderful second mom for my kids—more a friend than another "mom." As a result, I was also able to attract more things to be grateful for.

Whatever you're feeling is what you're attracting. Vibrations either attract or repel. If the vibrations are alike, then they attract. And if they're different, they repel. How this works is simple. You reach for a higher vibe thought and feeling.

But what about all the other people in your life? Will increasing your vibration change them or your relationship with them?

It's a possibility.

But you have to ask yourself, "Am I living my life for me or for them?" You are the only one living your life. In this moment, this is it. This is your choice. What is *your* choice?

I'm assuming that you choose to live your life. Great! Now, let me explain what will happen with all the other people in your life. Just as you have made a choice, they can also. Four scenarios can happen.

First, your vibration rises, and the other person chooses to raise their vibration, and you remain friends doing higher-vibe stuff. In addition, new friends will come into your life who are at this higher vibration.

Second, your vibration rises, and the other person chooses to stay at the old vibration. This person chooses to leave the relationship. This can happen without drama and trauma. One day, you just sort of notice that this person is no longer calling you.

Third, your vibration rises, and the other person chooses to stay at the old vibration. However, this time the person chooses to create drama and trauma. You have a choice here. Stay at your high vibration, or...

Fourth, you choose to lower your vibration to match the temper tantrum or guilt trip chosen by the other person. If you choose this, your relationship is "saved," but are you truly being who you choose to be? Don't worry—it doesn't have to be permanent. You can choose a higher vibration at any time.

Dear Future Lover,

I just noticed something. Do you ever think one thing and then all of a sudden BAM! A new awareness pops into your head that completely changes how you looked at that thing?

This is what happened today. I just realized that I lowered my vibration when I was engaged to my ex. Voluntarily. Ugh. You see, I'd been meditating for about six years. But once I started dating my ex, I thought I was too calm, and I didn't want to feel this way. Stupid, right? Anyway, I made the conscious choice to stop meditating.

It wasn't until today that I realized I had chosen to lower my vibration so that I fit better with him. Can you believe I was so silly? By the way, my headaches got a lot worse, but it took making this connection to give up trying to please others instead of myself. We understand it when we understand it.

You may wonder why I was even dating him. I had my eye on the wrong goal. I wanted to be married. He offered, and he filled many of my "qualifications.". I should have been more focused on having something like the amazing relationship you and I are going to have.

I know that I'll choose differently this time around. I'm choosing to do what's in my best interest. And if this relationship will help me be a better me, then I'm all for it. And if you don't already meditate, I hope you'll at least be open to the possibility.

Love,

J

So, what actually happened?
How did this letter influence the outcome?

(Truth be told, this letter wasn't in the original journal. The realization happened recently, and I felt the need to include this letter. But that will be our secret!)

Bruce meditates in his own way. To me, it looks like he's zoning out, and this is where he gets his invention ideas.

Together, we've started meditating with music and focusing on the feelings we desire. We sometimes meditate for as much as an hour and a half at a sitting. And it has made a huge difference in our lives. We are more loving and accepting. We disagree less and are more accepting of the other's ways of doing things. And my headaches occur much less often. We're allowing each other to be who each of us chooses to be.

Chapter 21

THE HIGH VIBES

Ease Is Found at Love, Peace, and Gratitude

If I'd used a template for these letters, perhaps I'd start each with something like this: *I'm grateful that your arms gently surround me, filling me with love. I'm grateful you're in my life making it even better. I'm grateful that we get along so well. I'm grateful that we accept each other for who we are.* You get the idea.

When my daughter, Shoshanna, started her *Dear Future Lover* journal, she started with gratitude. (Perhaps by the time this book is published, she'll have met him.)

What? She started with love and gratitude? What happened to working her way up the scale of feelings? That's what she's been doing for the past eight years. Before that, she was filled with depression, anxiety, and oppositional defiance. She certainly wouldn't desire to have a vibrational match with someone who vibrated at that level. Now, she has only a bit of the anxiety left, and that's rapidly diminishing. While she had relationships during that time, she recognized that she wasn't ready for "the one" until recently. She is now the happiest person I know, and she feels that she's ready to meet him.

So, how did these higher vibrations play into this change? Keep your eye on the long-term goal. For Shoshi, the long-term goal was to feel the love. After all, she's all about love and happiness. She just needed to catch up with her goal and, along the way, get out of a seven-year relationship, into another, and out of that one. Most importantly, she learned to love herself.

So, what is it about love, peace and gratitude that is so vital? These are some of the highest vibrations. If you can feel love, peace, and gratitude for everything—even the things that aren't so great—and actually feel the sensation, it will truly work for you.

Love is the yummy feeling you get that is like a snuggle or hug. Imagine the feeling pouring into you from the Universe. Feel it as it builds inside your body and spills out of you. When you choose to feel love in this way, you never have to worry about someone draining you, because you are constantly being filled from the Universe. Are you willing to be open to love? Here's a shortcut trick. Say, "I allow." Then imagine the love pouring into you.

Peace is that moment when "it" clicks. There isn't any pull to the past or the future. It just is. The body is relaxed and willing to receive whatever you are willing to allow.

Gratitude is about feeling grateful in the moment no matter what. Pre-gratitude is about feeling grateful for something that has yet to happen. You are grateful for it before it happens and this pulls what you are grateful for into your reality.

Imagine you're a kid, and you're given a red bike that you've wanted for a long time. It wasn't a little desire. It was a *big* desire. All you could talk about was that red bike, how you'd ride it every day, how you could run errands for your mother, how you were tired of sharing your sister's bike, how fast you'd be able to go. You could imagine the independence and sense of fun and freedom you would have when you had the bike. Your imagination went on and on with all that was possible!

When you received that bike, did you offer an off-handed "thanks"? Or did enthusiasm sneak through? Did your gratitude explode from your inner being, showering everyone within a hundred miles with the attitude of gratitude?

That's what I'm talking about. *That's* the difference—the sensations you send out into the world start within you.

And here's a clue…you can say (and feel) the attitude of gratitude *before* you ever get whatever you're thankful for. That's right! When you start feeling grateful, the universe says, "Oh, you want things to be grateful for. No problem—your wish is my command. Here you go!" You literally activate your inner magnet inside that will pull more things to you to be grateful for.

It's a vibration thing. Like attracts like. If you're vibrating at a gratitude speed, the Universe just wants to give you more to be grateful for.

Now, pause for a moment. Do things always show up the way you thought they would? Not at all. The red bike could have been different from the one you imagined. Your parents may have found a used bike at a garage sale and painted it red. Or you were imagining a three-speed bike and your parents splurged on a 10-speed one. Perhaps you did chores or got a job to earn money to help pay for it. Or some other way of feeling freedom and fun shows up.

When you ask for something and follow it with lots of heartfelt gratitude, the Universe will move mountains to give you what you're truly feeling.

Here's the conundrum. Sometimes what we are feeling (really, truly feeling on the inside) doesn't match up with what we say. To the outside world, it sounds as if you want *X*, but to your inside world (your feelings) you're saying something else altogether. Guess what? *Whatever you feel on the inside is what you'll get.* It's the default setting.

So why not preset your default setting to gratitude? Start feeling thankful for everything, all the time. When you think of something, find the gratitude that you'll have when you receive it. When you actually get it, let the gratitude spill out of you. When you remember it later, give thanks once, again.

When things don't go right, look for what you *can* be grateful for about the situation. This will turn the situation around.

Remember what Shoshi did. She raised her vibration until she was feeling the love, peace and gratitude on an hourly and daily basis. This is more advantageous than attracting a depressing guy and then deciding to feel better. He wouldn't stick around long, because his depression wouldn't match her love, peace and gratitude.

Shoshanna first put her energy into where she wants to be. From this place she will be able to attract a guy who also vibrates at that level. Then her future lover will be attracted to her as a high-vibe being. The higher your vibration, the more ease you will have while you bring your book boyfriend to life, which will bring in a much higher vibration guy.

Dear Future Lover:

Have you ever heard of Melody Gardot? I just discovered her voice. She is a wonderful jazz singer and is easy to listen to—partly because of the smooth jazz, but mostly because the music doesn't drown out her voice.

Her story is amazing. She started singing at the age of 9, but at 19, she was hit by a car. During her year-long recovery, she used music to rebuild the neural pathways in her brain. Even though she lives with daily pain, Melody is creating the music of her life. (Cheesy wording, but hey, it fits).

So, what are you overcoming in your life?

For me, I could say headaches, but at times I'm not sure "overcoming" is the right word. As much as I don't like them, I've learned a lot and perhaps lead a different life because of what I've learned.

Actually, there is no "perhaps." I know my life is different and even better because of what I've learned. The journey within has helped me discover my truth—or at least the glimmer of more truth yet to be revealed.

I have a choice here. Talk about the downs of the headaches or what I'm grateful for regarding them. I choose—yes, I make the choice—to see and feel the gratitude. In fact, I find that more and more I ask myself, "I wonder how this will benefit me?" or "Where's the gift from this?" This approach really takes the sting out of the unfortunate "bad" things that happen.

Did you know that I had three weeks in August without headaches? The gratitude comes in because I was able to truly enjoy the feeling of the warm snuggle I associate with it. I even went bike riding.

Now, back to the gratitude...I'm grateful that:

I've learned about energy and how to shift it.

I've seen the need for help with pain and have a way to help others.

I set up the integrative medicine initiative at Children's Memorial Hospital.*

I was able to integrate western medicine and alternative forms of healing through the CMH program, and through the program, I'm starting at the Children's Hospital of Wisconsin. [My involvement in this program since fell by the wayside.]

Headaches are a warning signal about something I don't want to feel or look at. I'm grateful for the knowledge that, if I persist, look, and then let it go, the feeling of being trapped will pass—as well as the headache.

Headaches helped me survive my marriage. This seems very strange, because the marriage didn't work for a long time. The headaches didn't give me the energy—or perhaps stole my energy—so I could accomplish my goal of being married once. It wasn't until Anamika, an angel therapist, told me that, to get rid of my headaches, I had to get rid of my husband that I was even willing to look at the possibility of divorce, which for me (and him) was the right move.

I guess this is another way of saying the headaches are teaching me to face my problems "head on" instead of "sweeping them under the rug." Chuckle, chuckle. Do you see the joke? Rug = hair. I never put it together like this before. I guess it would make more sense if I had a wig, but you get the idea. By the way, I'm having fun swinging my ponytail as I listen to Melody Gardot's music and write to you.

Gratitude and love,

J

*Children's Memorial Hospital is currently known as the Ann & Robert H. Lurie Children's Hospital of Chicago.

So, what actually happened?
How did this letter influence the outcome?

Bruce loves music…in his way. He loves karaoke, whistling, and playing the piano. In fact, one of the highlights of our summers is a karaoke party with friends and family. I love listening to music. Believe me, you'd much rather listen to him sing karaoke than me, although he's taught me the fun in participating.

CHAPTER 22

FOLLOW THROUGH

Take the Next Tiny Step

Each tiny step that you're inspired to do—and actually *do*—counts as following through. Acknowledge "the greatness of you" as you walk, run, skip, jump, and roll into the next choice and then choose to do it. Just as you can make a different choice every 10 seconds, you can acknowledge the follow through in 10-second intervals.

Imagine writing in your *Dear Future Lover* journal for 10 seconds. It's flowing and you choose to write another 10 seconds. In fact, the writing is pouring out of your fingers! Thirty minutes have gone by. Then all of a sudden, it seems to dry up. Do you have more to say? Would you like to continue writing? What would it take to end the journal entry with just the "right" tone? All the possibilities are there. Which ones are you open to?

And what about the times you *don't* feel like writing? This is just a feeling, and you already know you can change your feelings.

At the beginning of the following journal entry, I set out to write. You can tell that my expectations were low. "OK. I've written something. Job done." But then, because I started, more spilled out. In fact, important information was revealed to my future lover—I get moods, have trouble with the kids, and I'm searching for something enlightening and loving. My journal wasn't all "happy social media posts that tell the world how wonderful life is." It included the hard feelings in the moment.

Yes, I know it's important to focus on what I *do* want. But there's nothing wrong with mentioning what's going on...even if it's in an unfavorable light. The trouble comes in when we repeat it over and over and can't leave it behind. That only reinforces its hold on us and keeps us stuck in the past.

Some people like rules and structures. Others prefer flexibility and being able to create from all the possibilities. Do what works for you. *But* (and this is a big but) are you open to allowing another possibility better than you ever imagined? Give yourself permission to try something in a new way, whether it's a new rule or a totally new creation.

By writing as I did, I gave myself permission for the journal entry to be something other than what I thought it should be. I gave myself some wiggle room. You can also. If something doesn't work, try something else without beating yourself up.

Are you willing to let go of all the "shoulds"? This is *your* journal. The only "shoulds" are those you place there. No one else is dictating what to do or how to do it, not even me. I'm only giving you suggestions. So, do what works for you.

Then recognize that you've followed through. Whenever you place your energy in the space of having your lover in your life (writing in the journal, focusing on the feelings of having your future lover, or something else), you've added another puzzle piece—you followed through. Sure, you don't have your future lover yet, but he's coming. And the higher your energy is while you're writing the journal, the easier the whole process is.

An interesting thing happens each time you follow through. You get used to the vibration that you create, and your body gradually begins to be comfortable with this new vibration. Soon, you'll be able to maintain the sensation for longer periods of time.

Dear Future Lover,

OK. I've written something. Job done.

As you can probably guess, I'm feeling rebellious. Overall, life is great, and I really don't have much to complain about, although my headaches have been continuous and worse than usual. It centers around my fear of saying "no," (I think). I know this sounds strange, but it's an aspect of pleasing others that's particularly troublesome—especially when I want to say "no" but have trouble. I guess you could say it's a tug-of-war inside my head.

Combine this with wanting to be liked, and you can see how JT's recent behavior, which is too awful to write about, is leading to these headaches. So, today's mantra is to "just do something."

At this point, I don't even care what I do, except read more novels. I've done lots of that to escape since he's been home on break.

So, in the mood I'm in, I've done something and written this letter.

Unfortunately, as my future husband, you'll be exposed to these moods and the children who give them life. On the other hand, by the time we meet, maybe I'll have a way to deal with them...something enlightened and filled with love.

Until then,

J

So, what actually happened?
How did this letter influence the outcome?

Bruce can (and does) speak to the kids when they're out of line and warn them of "stuff to come" if they keep it up, especially when they were younger. He's very supportive of me and insists that the kids be respectful. He's making a difference. He's even modeling for the kids what a caring, loving husband does.

As a chiropractor, my husband feels bad because he can't solve my headaches. However, he can give me temporary relief with adjustments. And of course, he's always ready to offer the magic of his hands with midnight adjustments…the chiropractic kind. And thus, he has become known as my naked chiropractor. (Get your mind out of the gutter! Did you know that this phrase comes from a belief that equates sex with something dirty—the gutter? The more you say it, the more power you give it. I think it's time to change that rule.).

As for the follow through, he just keeps plugging away, expecting something even better and more useful.

Chapter 23

REACH FOR A MORE USEFUL FEELING

Things Can Be Even Better

No matter what "it" is, something can always be more useful and more easily work for you. Some people go to the negative and feel that things will be worse. Others go to the positive and feel they can get better. What you vibrate is what you feel, and thus, what you bring into your experience.

Sometimes when supposedly negative things happen, we get stuck in the negative. But if we keep in mind that things can become more useful, we can turn the "negative" into stepping stones that lead to the better, so they work *for* you instead of *against* you. The difference is how you think of it and feel about it. Let's break down a few common phrases and see how they do or don't move you toward what works for you.

"I'm happy, but not satisfied" has a feeling of dissatisfaction. It allows you to fall back into looking for the problem and fixing it.

"Yes, but..." is demotivating. It plays into the limiting belief that "I'm not good enough, so why bother trying?"

"Can it be even better?" is okay, but still allows for a kernel of doubt.

"What would it take to be even better?" implies that it can be better and eliminates the doubt. It has a sense or feeling of

excitement. Working to manifest the end result and reaching for the better feeling leads to an outcome that works for you.

What you ask becomes a self-fulfilling prophecy. *What you expect, you get.*

Think of the last few books you read. Have you ever picked up a book and it just didn't "feel right" at that time, and then months later you picked up the same book, loved it and couldn't imagine why you had trouble with it before? It's all about what you felt. Was it comfort, anxiety, anger, love, or something else? The vibrations you experienced while reading, influence what you felt in that moment. We actually feel the feelings of the characters (and even the author's feelings), and that is part of what makes reading so enjoyable. The feelings match up with what we feel, or our feelings shift to what the book is projecting. (As a side note, my husband loves when I read sexy scenes, and he is the beneficiary of that mood.)

This feeling "thing" is important for your own writing. If the feelings you are going for aren't high vibe, then the writing won't be either. It may be worth it to put your writing aside, do something high vibe and then return to your writing. If that isn't an option, start your writing, all the while reaching for a higher vibe feeling. Let go of the moaning, groaning, and complaining. After all, you don't want more things to moan, groan and complain about.

From my own experience, the vibration of what I write is a reflection of my internal vibration while I'm writing, and I've found that it's just not worth writing if my vibration isn't high. That's right—I don't write until I can plug into my high vibration.

This doesn't mean I don't write. It *does* mean that I raise my vibration *before* I write.

I can change the vibration by stepping up to the plate and doing something else. Personally, what works for me is to do things like exercise, take a long walk, listen to epic music, meditate, read something inspirational, laugh, ask myself questions, or something else. The more I release and let go of old sensations that are just hanging around doing nothing but clogging me up, the lighter I feel. The process can take a couple of minutes or a maybe few hours.

Everything I do to prepare myself for a higher vibe writing experience is a part of the writing process. On a recent writing day, my computer shut down unexpectedly. I turned it back on, then accidentally deleted the document that held all my notes. At this point, I decided that I'd put it away for the night. I could have been upset with myself and the computer, but I felt grateful for the words that *would flow*.

The next morning, I could have been angry that I woke up at 5:30—way earlier than my alarm. But I knew that I could take advantage of the morning, and I was grateful for that.

So instead of being angry when the computer shut down, the document got deleted, or I woke up early, something different happened. I stayed in gratitude and allowed for something better.

And something better *did* happen. Writing without notes, the words flowed out of me. I'd been "pre-feeling" the gratitude for my writing to flow out of me. My own progress had been hindered by trying to follow the notes, which were no doubt dry anyway. Something more useful came from the gratitude. I felt lighter, the writing improved and flowed with ease.

Could you allow yourself to feel whatever you are feeling in this moment? Could you allow yourself to feel something better? And better than that? And even better than *that*? Just stay open to the possibilities.

Dear Future Lover,

I didn't always think of the positive side of things. It used to be that my negative mind would spin scenarios of all the dreaded things that I thought would happen. And once I got on this train, it was very difficult to get off. And then I learned energy healing and consciousness transformation. Somewhere along the way things shifted. I started looking at what was working and what would it take to work even more in my favor. This was like a breath of fresh air. My mind quieted and I started to look forward to all the possibilities. Now, I find it annoying when I'm around people who complain.

I know that you won't complain. You have a positive outlook...at least most of the time. We will truly enjoy our time together and we reach for more and more things that work for us. I wonder what those things will be?

J

So, what actually happened?
How did this letter influence the outcome?

My husband doesn't complain. In fact, he had a knee replacement two years ago and was a great patient. I like taking care of him and appreciated it when he asked for my help. He set his mind on being happy no matter what, and he keeps reaching for that.

Chapter 24

JUDGMENT

Let Go of Fixed Points of View
...Including Judgments

We judge to keep ourselves safe. We judge because we fear what might be or what was. The fear grips us and influences our choices. A judgment is a way we limit ourselves. By judging something, we cut off the possibilities.

What if there was a better way of being? There is—by coming from a place of curiosity. Once you're open to another possibility, more possibilities present themselves.

So, where are you limiting the possibilities in your life by judging rather than dropping judgment and being curious? If you were to drop all judgment, what possibilities could emerge?

Yes, *you* are the one doing the limiting. *You* are the one judging.

But, but, but.... I can hear you now. (Many clients and students have had the same reaction.) Everyone assumes that judging is good and right. It's how we know what to do and what *not* to do.

What if something else was possible? In truth, it's about what works or doesn't work.

Whenever you judge, you impose a fixed point of view, which keeps you from having free choice. The idea of *not* judging is to increase the possibilities from which to choose. Once you do this, you can be more aware of the truth without the emotional tugging of the judgment.

Let's look at this a bit deeper. When you judge, you are imposing the point of view that something is right or wrong, good or bad. What could life be like if you let go of judgment and could make a choice in the moment from observing what is actually in front of you, or from a feeling of knowing truth?

Personally, when I operate from this, everything inside of me settles down and I'm filled with a sense of ease. And from this place, I have true choice. Even when I talk about reaching for the better feeling, what I'm actually reaching for is the sensation that feels even more expansive and more at ease.

The next time you judge something as right/wrong or good/bad, try this simple exercise. It will shift your focus. For every judgment, look for what is "right" about what you are judging. For example, assume you don't like tattoos. You might judge them as being bad, and then assume that the person with the tattoo is also bad. However, if you can focus on a more expansive feeling, you'll be open to more possibilities. Notice the creativity of the design, or be amazed that someone could sit for a long time with a needle continuously poking into him.

If you can learn to accept things "as is," you'll feel less turmoil within you. The next time you judge something, take a mental step back and find the amazingness about whatever you judged. Then pay attention to how you feel. It's your life. They're your feelings. Go for the high vibe! And I can pretty much guarantee that being curious feels a whole lot better than constantly criticizing, which is actually what most judgment is.

Dear Future Lover,

I was excited to be invited to a party at someone's house. I even baked a banana cake. If you haven't tried one, you should—super yummy. Well, I'd had a headache all week and Dr. Matt had just adjusted me, so I was feeling good, but as soon as I got to the party, I was overwhelmed with the number of people (about 30), and I didn't know what to talk about.

I totally clammed up. After a half hour, I left. I would have so much preferred if I'd had your hand to hold. So, I came home and watched TiVo. It occurred to me that I was more comfortable watching "Criminal Minds" then attending a party. Something is twisted here.

It's not always about the number of people. Thursday, I was at a dinner for 500. My stepmother got an award for Woman of the Year. She was the first woman in nine years to get the award for her college real estate program. I have a strategy in large groups like that. I stay on the edges so I won't feel overwhelmed

Yet, I was freaked out by a party of 30 people in someone's home. Weird. Any ideas of what this may be about?

Well, that's it, other than something cute that Adam said. We were on our way downtown on Thursday and were talking about my stepmother. I mentioned that when she started dating my father, they were on the society page. The caption said, "GW and her new beau, JM." My dad got a kick out of it because he was used to being listed first. Adam then said, "I didn't know I had famous grandparents." It was very funny, although it doesn't translate well on paper. Oh well.

Time for bed. I hope you are sleeping well.

Love,

J

So, what actually happened?
How did this letter influence the outcome?

My husband has a party past, and I don't judge him for it. Instead, I appreciate that he can feel comfortable in a large group and thus help *me* to feel comfortable. If it's staying by my side or giving me a smile across the room, I can feel the nerves slip away and the calm relaxes me.

CHAPTER 25

BE YOU

Quit Compromising Against Yourself

When you make a compromise, you're making a tradeoff. Compromising is how people get along. It's a survival instinct to help us fit in with the "tribe." However, what if it's not? What if there were a more useful tribe for you…if only you would let yourself be *you*?

Take dating for example. Imagine you've come across that really hot "someone" and are willing to twist yourself in knots to make yourself attractive. The twisting yourself in knots is a compromise. You've given up who you are to please someone else. In the end, you don't fit together because you have trouble keeping up with this false version of you. Wouldn't it be better to be with someone who loves you for *you*?

Too often, we try to fit in and be the "perfect _____" to please others, while in the process, we give up a part of ourselves. Think of yourself as a small child. "You'll make Mommy happy if you get dressed, go to school, and behave for the teachers." But underneath, you don't really like those choices. You'd sort of hoped to stay home and paint. It's all done with good intentions. Mommy thinks she's doing what is best for you, but deep down, you're disappointed. And then you're even *more* disappointed when Daddy makes disparaging remarks about your painting. According to him, you should be playing sports or doing something mechanical.

Pretty soon, you start to live life as this other thing (obediently going to school and then coming home to play soccer) instead of you (painting). Over time, you even forget that you wanted to paint. This may not seem like a big deal, but it is. You are the one living your life and, as such, you could be living *your* life but *you've chosen* to live not as you.

Besides being disappointing, this can lead to your body rebelling (what's wrong with my body?), your inner being trying to be recognized (what's wrong with me?), your constant disappointment with yourself (why am I not good enough?), or something even more drastic. In short, something goes wrong (like a dis-ease) and you have no idea why because you've been living the lie so long that you can't even remember who you are deep down. You've lived your life just as you've been told to do. How far will you go to be someone you're not?

More important, how far will you go to be who you truly are? Let's assume that the past is the past and the future can be different, depending on this moment. In this moment...

- ♥ Are you willing to step up and live your life as who you truly are?
- ♥ Are you willing to discover who this is?
- ♥ Are you willing to get over your past and allow yourself to be the best you that you can be?
- ♥ Are you willing to be the best you in this moment?
- ♥ What is the best you in this moment?
- ♥ Who do you choose to be?
- ♥ Whatever feeling is gripping in your chest or throat right now, are you willing to release and let it go forever?

That gripping sensation was your resistance to being the best you. On an internal level, if you're willing to be someone who you haven't chosen to be before, this causes some discomfort. You have the choice to experience this feeling and then let it go so you can allow yourself to discover something that works for you. Or you can choose to hold onto the feeling and never do or be something else. It's not about what the sensation is. It's about your reaction to it.

So, instead of reacting to something, after it's done take a moment to ask yourself if what you're contemplating is a compromise against yourself. Ask:

- ♥ Does this help me to be my true self?
- ♥ Is this what I choose to be, have, or do?
- ♥ Is this something that will support me in the direction I choose to go? (Not *should* go.)
- ♥ Is this in my best interest without harming others? (Just disappointing someone isn't harming others.)

You don't have to please the world or even your tribe. Live your life and don't make compromises against yourself. Discover who *you* are and what *you* desire.

Your identity is yours, not someone else's perception or opinion of you. Are you willing to follow your dreams, even if no one else is cheering you along the way? Even if no one else agrees or disagrees with you?

You are the only you. *Be yourself.*

Dear Future Lover:

Do you ever feel that you compromise yourself? Dr. C, one of my teachers, says that compromising oneself is the root of illness. So, I've been looking at my own life to see what compromises I've made against myself—those times when my mouth said "yes" but my gut said "no."

I've had a few of those compromises (okay, a few more than a few), but don't worry—I'm cleaning them up. I'm cleaning me up. And do you know what? I'm happier. It's actually easier saying what I do want. It's easier being honest with myself... once I figured out what that was.

I still know how to compromise. You see, as long as it's not a compromise against myself, it's okay. It's still acceptable to compromise when the reason is right for me. If the overall reason is because I love you and want to show that love, then compromise is one way to do that.

For example, if you want chicken for dinner and I want fish, I'm happy making chicken, because I love you. However, sometimes you'll compromise my way so it won't be lopsided. The compromise against myself would be if the meal was made from wheat, since I blow up and swell if I eat too much wheat.

But there are ways around it. When Shoshi wanted spaghetti (her favorite) and I wanted fish (she hates it), I made both. Then we were both happy and could eat together as a family, which is more important than what we eat. It was a very white meal, especially when I served cauliflower with it.

I wonder why I do that—the color thing. Ideally, meals are multicolored, but every once in a while, they end up being monochrome. I'm sure color means something.

This happened when the kids were little also. I'd feel like wearing purple, so I would. Then I'd dress the kids. Later in the day, it would dawn on me that they were dressed in purple also. I know it means something, I just don't know what.

That's the way it is with signs from the Universe. I wonder how I'll know you. Will it be something you wear? I remember once saying to the Universe, "My partner will be wearing an orange shirt." A short while later, I attracted a man into my life who talked about being partners and his favorite color was orange. It took me a while to realize that I'd said it and it happened, but it was exciting to see the sign fulfilled.

So, why didn't the relationship last? He wasn't you. The word "pedestal" comes to mind. It seems selfish, but I want to be put on a pedestal. I know that you'll think I'm special. I'm even beginning to think that I'm special. I guess I had to get to the point where I thought it and felt it about myself before I could attract you into my life to mirror it back to me.

So, what am I mirroring back to you? Do you see the love? Do you feel it? I can. It feels as if my heart is expanding and growing beyond my chest cavity, filling the space within and around with misty sparkles. It's more than white. Rainbows of colors swirl around in a lazy pace. The more I feel this love, the more it grows, waiting to be entwined with yours, together becoming even more.

Can you feel it? Do you feel it as I write to you? Perhaps you feel this wave of love and have no idea where it's coming from. Well, it's me. Our higher consciousnesses know each other and will bring us together. This beacon of love light is shining from my lighthouse within, searching the world for you. Just you. I will know you because our heart energy will grow and intensify when we are together. With two, we will have the power of ten. Together, we will make the world—or at least our own worlds—a better place. Together, the strength of our love will shine through the fog, showing us the possibilities before us. The possibilities together powered by our love will be even more effective versions of ourselves.

I can feel the love. Can you?

Feeling you,

J

So, what actually happened?
How did this letter influence the outcome?

My husband encourages me to honor and respect myself. He never expects me to do something that is a compromise against myself. And in fact, he's joined me on the journey within to wash away what no longer serves us.

As for the slow bit, my husband is from the South. When he does something slower, such as eating dinner, or we have a misunderstanding, he says it's a North/South thing. He uses this excuse a lot.

And as for the idea of making the world a better place, Bruce started the Burn Solution Foundation to give his patented burn cream to the homeless, members of the military and victims of natural disasters.

If you would like to find out more about the Foundation, please go to www.burnsolutionfoundation.com. They are always accepting donations. I am sending pre-gratitude your way right now. Thank you.

Chapter 26

FEEL THE TRUTH

It's Only True Until It's Not

It's easier to give up judging when you know how to find truth, so let's start there. Have you ever thought about what truth *feels* like? Go back to a time when you knew something was true. You didn't think it *might* be, but you actually *knew* it. What did you feel in your body? Now, go to a time when you knew something was off. For example, you knew when someone was lying to you. What did you feel in your body at that time? Chances are the feeling wasn't the same for the two experiences.

Truth feels like an opening, relaxing expansiveness. It has a light and airy feeling often accompanied by an exhale. It may even be a tingle through your whole body. A truth makes you feel strong. In short, it works for you.

A lie feels just the opposite. Think of it as a gut punch causing you to contract or feel heavy. It makes you feel weak and doesn't work for you.

You may have different sensations that you recognize as truths and lies. Don't accept what I say as truth. Feel it for yourself. Know what your feelings are.

Here's a hint: Sometimes it's easier to feel the sensation if you stand with your knees loose (not locked), arms hanging at your side. When you feel your truth, your body may sway. Some people sway forward with the feeling of truth; others sway backward. Pay attention to your own body.

I'm frequently asked, "How can I trust the feeling when I'm not sure I'm feeling it?" That's a good question. Oops—"good" is a judgment. Let's try again. That's a question that opens the door to more possibilities, rather than saying, "I can't feel it."

Whenever you have a statement, you have only one choice. There isn't any wiggle room for something else. When you say, "I can't feel it," you're actually telling the Universe what you'd like, and the Universe gives you what you ask for—more experiences that prove you can't feel it. You get more experiences that reinforce the belief you have stated.

So, what would it take to feel truth and what works for you? Experiences. The more you can experience this, the easier it will be. Every time you have a choice (which, by the way, is very often), ask yourself if something feels expansive or contracted.

We are presented with choices all the time. What to eat, which way to drive or walk, which book to read, which party to go to (or not go to), which person to talk to, what to say, what time to set your date for, which date to choose, and so on. By paying attention to the feelings in your body, the choices become easier to make.

When you come to an intersection, you have many choices. Turn right or left. Go forward or backward. Turn around in a circle. Or just plain stop. Ask yourself, "If I turn right, what happens to my energy?" "If I go straight, what happens to my energy?"

Big point: The answer doesn't have to make sense. And very often, it doesn't. Pay attention to the feeling, and then follow the feeling of expansiveness. The more you do this, the louder the feeling will become and the easier it will be for you to recognize it. Pretty soon, you won't need to ask the full question. You'll just be getting the feelings.

Wait a minute—do it even if it doesn't make sense? Yes! Each choice leads to more possibilities and more choices. Going the way that you "should" go may lead you into an accident. But going the way that feels most expansive or light (but possibly doesn't make sense) may lead you past the perfect house you've been looking for but hadn't been able to find. And oh, that future lover? He's getting out of his car next door to that house.

The thing is we don't know everything, and by following the feelings, we're working with the Universe. The whispers of feelings are the Universe nudging us toward our dreams. Pay attention to what you are feeling.

The first couple of times you do this, you might get the thought that the Universe is playing with you, and you can't see why one choice is more useful than another. Keep with it. We don't always know *why* things are done. This is where trust comes in. Trust your feelings.

You get to choose to listen or not. However, if a feeling or thought keeps repeating, it's worth paying attention to, even if it's only to notice that you have an emotional attachment, aversion, or judgment and something needs to be released, neutralized, or cleared. The more you let go of, the easier it is to recognize the truth feelings because nothing is competing with the feeling. Releasing and letting go of the attachments or resistance to the feelings is like cleaning your glasses. You can see through dirty glasses, but it's easier to see through ones that are clean.

And, by the way, it's only true until it's not. Just as you can change your choices, the truth can change also. What? The truth can change? That's right. Depending on what we're thinking and feeling, along with the emotional attachments or aversions we're holding onto, the truth may show up differently if something else changes. Remember when women wore long dresses with low bodices? Their breasts were on display, but their ankles were covered. Apparently, it was scandalous to show your legs. What was true then isn't true now.

Dear Future Lover,

Have you ever experienced that sense of knowing? You automatically know if something is true or not. I know that when we meet, I'll have that knowing feeling. My whole body will relax and give a big sigh.

Most of the time, I'm so keyed up that it feels as if my shoulders are in my ears and my back is ramrod straight. This is the opposite of how I will feel when we meet.

Thank you for helping me to relax and be open in my life, our relationship, and with my desires. Thank you for allowing me to feel the peace within me. Thank you for bringing out the best in me. Thank you for acknowledging my powers.

You see, I've spent so long trying to please others that I sometimes don't recognize what would please me. And along with this, I don't believe that I can do what others are telling me that I can do—specifically, the energy healing. I know I get great results, but something is holding me back from believing in myself. Thank you for believing in me and showing me how to believe in myself.

Love you soon,

J

So, what actually happened?
How did this letter influence the outcome?

When we met, I was instantly interested in Bruce, and I moved my chair so I could be closer to him and hear him more clearly. The following night, while at dinner with a group, a woman was sitting at the head of the table between us. I thought, "This doesn't work for me." That's when I moved my chair to sit next to him.

He also felt the initial recognition and saw something in me. We were comfortable together from the beginning.

But here's is a funny story about how our truths didn't agree. On our second "date," I told him that I'd previously said, "My next husband is going to be a chiropractor." (And I initially said that before I went through my divorce.) Bruce was quick to say, "I'm never getting married again." I paused, felt the sensations in my body and then boldly said, "Well, I am." He just believed his truth, because he was operating from fear. I knew my truth because I'd asked my body. I never pressured him to get married…and here we are.

And as for knowing truth, while Bruce was in the Army, he knew that he needed to be a chiropractor and became one. In fact, in the 1970s, he had one of the largest integrative offices in the U.S. Other medical doctors worked for him. His favorite part of the practice was testifying in court, something that scares other doctors, but fed right into his showmanship. Normally, one wouldn't think that becoming a doctor would lead to showmanship, but his path did.

Chapter 27

NEUTRALITY

The Art of Being at Peace

We boost the effectiveness of our possibilities through neutrality. This is when no singular possibility has a hold on you. You have neither an attachment nor a resistance to it. You're free to examine it, and then let it go to allow another possibility.

Imagine having a strong opinion. It consumes you. You're always aware of it. It's all you talk about. The opinion could be something you are for or against—it doesn't matter. It's almost as if the opinion has a hold on you. You make plans based on the opinion. You do things because of the opinion. You *don't* do things because of the opinion. You get the idea—the opinion owns you.

Neutrality is about letting go of the hold so you have the freedom to make a choice (if you choose to have it or not is up to you), but when you aren't holding so tightly to that opinion, other ideas (possibly more useful ones) can arise. From this point of neutrality, all options are available.

Think about the first contact you'll have with your future lover. Did you feel something in your body? What sensation did you have? It doesn't matter what your answers are. What matters is the feeling or sensation you actually experienced…even if it was a little flutter of excitement or a gut punch of fear. And all you were doing was thinking of meeting this lover.

Whatever that sensation is, are you willing to neutralize it? Are you willing to release and let it go forever? This sensation is just an emotional hiccup, and you're telling the Universe that you're willing to let go of the hold of that emotional hiccup. By letting go of it, you'll actually open up more possibilities. You don't have to choose the possibilities if you don't desire them, but if you hold onto strong feelings—which show up as strong opinions—you are limiting your choices.

It's as easy as asking: "Am I willing to (let go, release, destroy, un-create, harmonize, neutralize, incinerate) _____? The blank can be filled in with:

- ♥ "whatever gets in the way of me being, having, or doing _____?"
- ♥ "whatever that is?"
- ♥ "anything and everything that gets in the way of ___?"

Once you feel neutrality, you will wonder why you held onto your viewpoints so strongly. You will feel at peace no matter what. This is a true art that is worth cultivating.

Dear Future Lover,

I had so much fun tonight at the Integrative Touch for Kids benefit. I was relaxed and able to talk with people. After dinner (during the live auction) I was talking with Sandy about flipping energy. I did a mini-session with her, then with her husband, then with his cousin. I was moving my fingers to the beat of the auctioneer's voice—VERY QUICKLY.

Sandy wanted to play in improved communication and confidence. Her sense of overwhelm shows up as body shakes and low body temperature. After our session, these all but disappeared—the shakes were gone and she felt warm.

Her husband, a lawyer, set his intention at having more business. As I was finishing, I had the thought (which I didn't verbalize), "I'll add more energy so he can handle the increase in business." After I was done, I asked him what felt different. He said he felt more energized. Yes! The cousin had a stomachache. I could see his body posture change when the ache went away.

Oh, I forgot to tell you something great! When I was playing in the energy with Sandy, she said she saw white light as I waved my arm, and my body was all white light. This was the first time she saw white light! She also felt the joy!

This stuff is so cool. I can't wait to try it with you.

Love,

J

So, what actually happened? How did this letter influence the outcome?

Interestingly, the lawyer in the letter above got very busy, and he was very grateful that I'd added that energy to the outcome. And my friend, Sandy, used this Dear Future format to find a new job. After only one letter, the new job found her.

Bruce is open to my shifting the energy. In fact, he's one of the first people to tell others about how I helped him. He's a great cheerleader for me.

CHAPTER 28

SIGNS

Pay Attention to the Signs Around You

The world is a mirror. The Universe is always giving us signs, nudging us in the direction of our dreams and our feelings about those dreams. Anything and everything can be a sign. Our part is to stay open to the possibilities, and then notice what draws our attention.

A few years before meeting my husband, I was engaged to another man (oops). His dog had my name, Judy, and she was so important to him that, during his divorce, he fought for shared custody! This wasn't an issue by itself, but, in this case, he fought constantly with his adult daughter over who would take care of the dog. I realized that here was a female (the dog with my name) who was so important to him that he'd fought for her, yet he wouldn't care for her. Was this to be *me*?

I was unsure as to what to do, so I asked the angels for guidance. I remember standing in my back hall, looking at the ceiling (as if the angels were there), saying, "Please give me a sign that's so big I'll have to trip over it."

The next morning, I went to my doctor, who is also a friend, and she told me, "The only thing wrong with you are your emotions about the fiancé." She then clamped a hand over her mouth and her eyes popped wide open. She said, "I wasn't going to say that! It just came out."

I assured her that it was the perfect message I'd asked for.

To make sure that I was in alignment with the message, I meditated and journaled until it felt like I was comfortable with every aspect of the decision. I then wrote a letter to my fiancé outlining the breakup and how he deserved someone who loved him for him.

Before printing the letter (this is important), I went to make dinner for him. Later, he asked to talk. He said, "Do you want to break up?" I was shocked!

But I'd done the preparation work and knew what I was feeling.

It was the gentlest breakup ever. We hugged and even went out the next night as friends. It didn't get tumultuous until others started weighing in with their view of how it "should" be.

In the end, I'd asked for a sign, and then I made sure I was in alignment with the feelings. I didn't even have to do the breaking up. He initiated it.

But I assume you aren't breaking up with anyone right now. You're looking for your future lover. So, what signs would you like to set up? Will he love orange or purple? Will he say something? Will *you* say something? You can set up whatever sign feels expansive.

A few days before I wrote this chapter, I slipped in the bathroom and ended up doing the splits. I had a headache for two days. Thankfully, I'm healthy and I've been doing yoga. And it certainly came in handy that my husband is a chiropractor.

Yes, there was water on the floor. That was the logical explanation. But what was the sign? My right leg (the male side of the body, associated with success and career) slid forward, while the left leg stayed behind (left is the female side and is associated with emotions). Dr. Jahner, my mentor, asked me where I was deferring, delaying, or ignoring my future possibilities out of consideration for the choices of those I love, which are anchored in who I *was* instead of who I *am*. He explained that I'm growing and changing (including getting this book out into the world), and the loved ones in my life are having a hard time keeping up. I was more concerned about them than with my growth, and this was slowing me down.

Signs are all around us. They may show up as a billboard, an overheard conversation, a song that pops into your head, someone interacting with you, something happens to you, etc. Pay attention and notice what draws your attention. This noticing is a big deal. It's the light bulb that goes off in your consciousness that brings your attention to something important.

What to do about the sign? The only thing you can change is yourself. Thus, if you recognize something as a sign, look deep within and become aware of what you're thinking, feeling, or doing that would attract whatever you noticed. Change your thoughts, feelings, or actions if you choose to have something different show up. Or recognize the sign as what you asked for and give thanks.

Remember, *notice the world around you*. It's speaking to you all the time.

Dear Future Lover,

It's ironic, my writing these letters. It began as an idea while reading The Pull of the Moon. Then Felissa, a friend, and I saw Daddy Long Legs, a play about writing letters and falling in love. Tonight, we saw She Loves Me, another play about writing letters to a stranger and falling in love. I swear I didn't know what either play was about before we saw them.

> The Universe works in mysterious ways. I wonder where this is all leading. I'm anxious to find out.
>
> Love,
>
> J

So, what actually happened?
How did this letter influence the outcome?

I'm not sure how this letter influenced my relationship with Bruce other than I was reassured that letters were the way to go. This highlighted the fact that writing letters (the thing I was doing) would lead to finding my lover.

CHAPTER 29

INFINITE BEINGNESS

Expand and Be All of You

My experience with the client in this chapter's letter was profound. As I coached her over six months, I was impressed with her desire to never play the victim and to be her best regardless of her circumstances. She taught me that I can make a difference if I accept my gifts of coaching and removing energetic roadblocks. In this case, my gift was to help a difficult transition be filled with love.

If we expand and allow ourselves to be the infinite beings that we truly are, then all possibilities are available to us. If we try to limit ourselves to make other people feel comfortable, we are limiting our gifts. Wanting to please others forces us into a smaller space. Ah, but remember: It's only true until it's not. You can make a new choice and expand.

We are infinite beings. "Infinite" means that we go on and on without ending. Obviously, our bodies have limitations, but our energy doesn't. Think of your energy as vibrating within you but still moving outward—as big as your house, your city, your state, your country, the world, to the stars and beyond. Once you've consciously expanded and become aware of how infinite you are, you'll be able to see things in a different light. Something that was so important to you when you were acting small is only a blip on your radar when you are expanded.

Yes, *acting small*. When we act small, we are trying to squish into a box. Imagine living in a refrigerator box. It's big enough so you might be semi-comfortable and not even realize you're in a box. But now imagine trying to fit your body into a shoebox. Your body would soon protest about the constrictions and pressure.

This is what happens when we're not being our expansive selves, accepting and playing with the gifts we do have. Our bodies protest.

Live the life you were meant to live, complete with the gifts you have. Limiting yourself is like saying other people are sick, so you should also be sick. When we think of it in terms of health, it seems ludicrous. It's as if we can't be healthy because others are not.

Why should it be any different for developing our gifts? If your gift is to be a painter, be the best painter you can be. If your gift is to be an accountant, be the best accountant you can be. If your gift is to be a dancer, be the best dancer you can be. But is any one of these gifts all of you? No! You're so much more.

Always be your best self no matter what others do to make you small. Often, others would like you to stay as they know you, because it's familiar to them. They don't want you to improve too much. They *say* they want you to improve, but subconsciously, they're trying to stuff you into a box that they see you in. They may act up, pick fights, fail to show up, and more. It's their reaction. It's their choice.

And just as they have choices as to how to act, so do you. If you set your sights on living as your expansive self by developing your gifts, know that others may want something different. That doesn't mean you have to agree with them.

This is how it works. As you accept and develop your gifts, your personal vibration rises. Or is it the other way around? Your vibration rises and then you develop your personal gifts? Either way, you're becoming your best self.

The people who could see you at one vibration now freak out because they can't find you in this new vibrational space. They have choices—join you and raise their vibration, leave, or try to bring you back down to their level.

Let's look at it in a different way. Let's say your vibrational level is usually anger, and through your choices and decisions, you're now vibrating at confidence and pride. The people who liked you when you were angry don't want you to feel better and will try to pull you down, because they can't imagine that you are no longer like *them*. You decide whether you'd like to slide back into anger. But likely, once you've tasted confident pride, you won't want the anger. In fact, you may be searching for something even more expansive. And along the way, your friends may change, and there's nothing wrong with that.

If you decide to return to the anger, you'll quickly realize that you're squishing into a smaller version of yourself. This creates tension and pressure, and you'll truly feel it.

The choice is yours. In this moment, will you accept all of you…including the gifts you are and the gifts you can be to the world? Make a choice. Are you willing to live inside a box? Or now, in this moment, will you accept all of you?

Life is a series of small choices. What choices are you are making?

Dear Future Lover,

The energy surely changed last week when I decided to accept my gift. I shifted the energy around it and things changed immediately. Finally, I was able to cut my hair. At first, I didn't like it, but now that I've had time to play with it, I like it. (More about the hair decision later.)

Other shifts—three men came up to me and talked for a more extensive time. I was even interested in one. He was a gentleman. Are you him?

Work-wise, things are more positive. More clients and more writing.

Tuesday, I had an energy session with Robin, a new client. My sister asked me if I could help Robin feel more comfortable as she dealt with a brain tumor and the resulting treatment. A side effect of what I do is that the person feels relaxed, so I agreed. I'd just received a very nice music CD and I played it as I flipped energy, which I chose to do silently. The session was about an hour, and Robin and her husband both benefited. At the end of the hour, I just held the space of love, and they held each other and cried. It was beautiful. When I left there, I felt so full of love, more than ever before!

Today, my sister called and said that the doctors think Robin has a week to live. I'll go to the hospital again tomorrow.

JT's Eau Clair wrestling team is here tonight. They say it's the highlight of their season to stay here before the Wheaton tournament. The kids are very nice and polite. I can see small town grace in each of these kids. It certainly is different than my home town.

Time for bed.

Love,

J

So, what actually happened?
How did this letter influence the outcome?

Robin, lived another six months, and I visited her many times. She called me her "spiritual therapist." One of the last things we did was to set up signs she'd send to her husband after she passed over. Shortly after she died, I got a text from her husband. He'd seen the sign that morning, and it was super-charged with something even more personal than we'd set up beforehand.

My husband totally supports my expanding and being everything I can be. I do the same for him.

CHAPTER 30

PERSONAL RESPONSIBILITY

It's Your Life. Take Responsibility for It.

Enough of the serious stuff—let's have some fun! Are you ready to play a game? Let's play the Blame Game, where you get to blame everyone and everything for whatever is going on in your life. Everything is someone else's fault. You're a victim of someone or something. It's easy to play, and it's easy to slip into victim mentality.

"Victim mentality" means you don't have to accept responsibility. The winner of the Blame Game is the one with the most stuff going wrong.

This sounds like fun. You get to fit in and complain to your heart's delight. But the more you complain, the more the Universe gives you to complain *about*. That's just the way it works. The Universe wants to give you what you desire, what you're focusing on—in this case the complaining and blaming.

Or are you ready for something else? Are you ready to stop complaining and change your perspective? It's easy. Just stop complaining and blaming. That's it. Take responsibility for everything in your life. Look for your contribution to whatever happens.

It's all about how you react and how you *choose* to react. Yes, things happen and people do stuff. But where do you focus?

What's that? You say the last guy you dated was mean and yelled a lot? What was your contribution? You chose to go out with him. Did you ignore the grumbling feeling in your stomach before you accepted the date? Did you accept the date just because he was someone to go out with, when in reality you never liked him to begin with? When he started yelling, did you choose to leave, or did you sit there and listen to him?

Make choices that benefit you. Just because you made the choice to go out with the "meany" doesn't mean you have to stay with him. You can make a new choice. You can take responsibility for what you do.

Can you also take responsibility for what you think and feel? Yes!

Look at this from a new perspective. Can you give this guy a little wiggle room to be in a bad mood? (You don't have to be with him while he is.) Can you decide to treat yourself kindly? (Quit talking about it and reliving the experience.) Can you let go of the story as it was? (Stop giving it power over you. Find something positive to say about it.)

Talk about life as you desire it to be. For example, if you want love in your life, then think, feel, and do things that will boost that feeling. Your viewpoint is up to you. What you talk about is up to you. What you think about is up to you. This is what taking personal responsibility is all about.

You can live your life by complaining and playing the blame game *or* you can choose to take responsibility for your life. The choice is up to you.

The following letter illustrates how I started whining and then took responsibility for it...

CHAPTER 30

PERSONAL RESPONSIBILITY

It's Your Life. Take Responsibility for It.

Enough of the serious stuff—let's have some fun! Are you ready to play a game? Let's play the Blame Game, where you get to blame everyone and everything for whatever is going on in your life. Everything is someone else's fault. You're a victim of someone or something. It's easy to play, and it's easy to slip into victim mentality.

"Victim mentality" means you don't have to accept responsibility. The winner of the Blame Game is the one with the most stuff going wrong.

This sounds like fun. You get to fit in and complain to your heart's delight. But the more you complain, the more the Universe gives you to complain *about*. That's just the way it works. The Universe wants to give you what you desire, what you're focusing on—in this case the complaining and blaming.

Or are you ready for something else? Are you ready to stop complaining and change your perspective? It's easy. Just stop complaining and blaming. That's it. Take responsibility for everything in your life. Look for your contribution to whatever happens.

It's all about how you react and how you *choose* to react. Yes, things happen and people do stuff. But where do you focus?

What's that? You say the last guy you dated was mean and yelled a lot? What was your contribution? You chose to go out with him. Did you ignore the grumbling feeling in your stomach before you accepted the date? Did you accept the date just because he was someone to go out with, when in reality you never liked him to begin with? When he started yelling, did you choose to leave, or did you sit there and listen to him?

Make choices that benefit you. Just because you made the choice to go out with the "meany" doesn't mean you have to stay with him. You can make a new choice. You can take responsibility for what you do.

Can you also take responsibility for what you think and feel? Yes!

Look at this from a new perspective. Can you give this guy a little wiggle room to be in a bad mood? (You don't have to be with him while he is.) Can you decide to treat yourself kindly? (Quit talking about it and reliving the experience.) Can you let go of the story as it was? (Stop giving it power over you. Find something positive to say about it.)

Talk about life as you desire it to be. For example, if you want love in your life, then think, feel, and do things that will boost that feeling. Your viewpoint is up to you. What you talk about is up to you. What you think about is up to you. This is what taking personal responsibility is all about.

You can live your life by complaining and playing the blame game *or* you can choose to take responsibility for your life. The choice is up to you.

The following letter illustrates how I started whining and then took responsibility for it...

Dear Future Lover,

Do you ever find that things get done more consistently when you have a schedule? I don't mean the "locked into a certain time" type of schedule. But more the "I'm used to doing it" type. I enjoy variety, but with variety comes more variety. Things just get jumbled up. Not in a bad way. This is another way of saying that I haven't written so often since San Francisco, and now Eau Claire. It's been a traveling week.

We got here at 1:45 this morning. Jessi, a friend of my boys, had a diving meet, so we were supposed to leave at 6:30 p.m., but Adam was doing his laundry, so we didn't pick her up until 7. The drive was smooth, and we stopped at a nice restaurant for dinner, which took an hour and was tons yummier than a fast food place that I can't eat at anyway.

We are staying at a Days Inn, a cheap motel near JT's townhouse. JT booked it on Hotels.com so it didn't go smoothly, but the place is clean. Of course, the walls are thin, and we slept for about five hours.

I feel like I'm whining, so I'll sign off for now. Just so you know, when I get overtired, I'm good for a while, but when I crash, I can get a tad whiny, which I don't like at all. And I don't even like to write it down for fear that I'm setting an intention.

So, for today's intention: To enjoy something in everything. I'm not sure how this will show up, but it will be fun watching.

Lots of Love,

J

So, what actually happened?
How did this letter influence the outcome?

Bruce almost never complains, and he takes responsibility for the things in his life. He chooses to be happy and knows that complaining and blaming are the opposite of happiness.

CHAPTER 31

FORGIVENESS

Forgive Yourself and Others

Now it's time to take responsibility for your own happiness. You can decide if you want to forgive yourself and others.

Think of a painful incident. You're the one feeling the resentment, embarrassment anger, or other hurtful feelings. Whoever else is involved with the incident isn't feeling what you are—they're carrying their own stuff. But you don't have to continue hurting yourself. If you choose to forgive, you'll increase your happiness and a huge weight will be lifted from your shoulders.

Forgiveness is about letting something go and not allowing it to have an attachment to you. It's the attachment to you that restricts your freedom and choices. After all, if you don't forgive, you're holding onto the fear, anger, disrespect, and so on. And as an added bonus, the more you *don't* forgive, the more you hold yourself back, feel hurt, weak, and powerless, and run at a lower vibration.

For your own freedom, forgive and move on. Let it go.

And if it's something you need to forgive about yourself, it's the same process. Give yourself permission to not be perfect all the time. Chalk it up to a learning experience and decide that the next time "that" happens you'll make a different choice. This is where you choose whether you want to feel expansive or be right.

How do you forgive? Here are some ideas:

- ♥ <u>Find something in the other person that you *can* forgive.</u> For example, imagine the other person as a little child. Forgive the child. It's about the feeling of you forgiving.
- ♥ <u>Question what happened.</u> Perhaps what you thought was happening was actually something else. Stay open to asking questions about the incident and accept whatever you hear. If you immediately jump to conclusions, you're putting up a brick wall. Questions give you fluidity and allow for change.
- ♥ <u>Be at peace.</u> Neutrality is very powerful because it helps you let go of any attachments or resistance you are holding onto, which will ultimately limit your choices. (Chapter 39 about Relationships offers a great exercise to help you with this.)
- ♥ <u>Be grateful.</u> Find *something* to be grateful for. Write a list of all the things you're grateful for about the situation you're having trouble forgiving.
- ♥ <u>Make the decision and choice to forgive.</u> It's that simple. Are you willing to give up the feeling? Are you willing to find the space where you *do* forgive? And what would feel even more expansive? Ultimately, it's your choice to feel lighter or not.

This doesn't mean that you have to *forget*. Forgiveness removes the emotional charge from the memory. Forgetting or not forgetting is a different choice.

Dear Future Lover,

What are you not forgiving in your life? Is it worth it to hold onto whatever is keeping you stuck?

It took a lot of work for me to forgive my ex-husband. Everyone told me that I should be outraged because of his mistress. But when I got the detective's report, I realized that I was more upset that he was pulling weeds for her than that he was cheating! It struck me as weird, and I was hurt, but not terribly upset, as we'd already decided to separate. (Over the next years, I'd found out that the relationship had been going on for years.)

When I wrote my list of things I was grateful for about the situation, I realized that I was very grateful that she took him off my hands. As soon as I wrote it, it felt as if my entire body had a huge sigh and relaxed. From then on, I was grateful for her.

And as for forgiving my ex? He is who he is, and I can't change him. All I can do is let him be him...far away from me.

Did I tell you about this "far away" bit? I said a prayer as the divorce was ending. I asked God to keep him far away from me and the kids. A year and a half later, he moved to China. That's pretty far!

Anyway, this whole forgiveness stuff is an ongoing exercise. I know that I'll screw up, and you will too. I hope that we'll be able to forgive each other and move on.

Love you,

J

So, what actually happened?
How did this letter influence the outcome?

My husband jokes that my prayers are so powerful that he'd better watch it, or he'll end up on Mars! And as for forgiveness, we're doing great.

Chapter 32

HABITS

Create New Habits

We do things because they're comfortable and familiar. Even things that we view as uncomfortable are actually comfortable to our subconscious, because they're familiar. This is because we run on memorized patterns. We repeat things because we've done them often in the past, so we know what to expect. These things become habits.

We form habits when we do something over and over. Some habits are helpful, and some have room for improvement.

Have you heard the story of the new wife who was cooking a roast for dinner? She cut off both ends of the roast before she put it in the pan. When her husband asked her why, she said, "That's how my mother does it." Her husband urged her to ask her mother why this was done. The mother replied, "That's the way Grandma taught me." So, they called Grandma to ask her why she did it that way. Grandma laughed and said, "The pan was too small."

The more you do something, the more it becomes a habit, even if you don't know the reason. To change a habit, you need to be willing to be or do something differently—over and over—thus forming a new habit.

When we try something new, there's an element of breaking free from past actions. This can create a moment (or many moments) of anxiety or fear which, by the way, can feel the same as excitement. It just has a different label, and thus influences how we interpret the sensation.

Are you willing to try something new? Are you willing to break free from your limiting past? If you're willing, it can be done!

One of my favorite ways to break into something new is to imagine my desire as if it was a wacky cartoon. (Can you tell I grew up with Looney Tunes?) Anyway, I visualize what I would like to happen in cartoon form, and the crazier the cartoon, the more powerful it seems to be.

For example, while I was walking one day, my hip began to hurt. I imagined Bugs Bunny as a surgeon operating on my hip. Daffy Duck was assisting. They pulled out a bedroom dresser, a large hammer, and various other items. By the time the "surgery" was done, the hip pain was gone…and I was laughing.

One reason it worked is because I let go of expecting things to be a certain way in a certain time, as I would have if I'd hooked into the habit of healing a certain way. I was open to the situation being different, but I didn't place limitations on it. How and when it happened were left up to something other than me and what I could imagine. I was open to things being different. I was willing to walk on the wacky side.

Dear Future Lover,

Remember when I told you about releasing/neutralizing "receiving?" What? I didn't? Let me backtrack a little.

Annette suggested that being able to receive is one of humanities greatest blocks. I was sure it was affecting me too. So, I set my neutralizing topic to "receiving," after all if I had issues with it, then how will I ever receive you into my life? You're not a habit yet, but I'm hoping.

The whole subject must have been percolating for a few days, because things were already shifting before Annette even suggested it. On Sunday, Jahner asked if I wanted to work together on Wednesday. Monday, Tad said he was available on Wednesday to give a massage if I wanted. Today, Jen said that she was thinking of calling me on Wednesday to see if I wanted to release, but her schedule filled up before she could call.

Everything on Wednesday. Coincidence? Probably not. Although I did do the releasing of "receiving" on Wednesday with Kate (I brought in reinforcements because I could feel the resistance. We were done after an hour, and the underlying issue seemed to be related to me not feeling worthy of receiving. Could I let that go of the habit of feeling unworthy of receiving? You bet!

At this point, Kate and I seemed to get stuck, so she suggested I matrix the whole thing. I did. At one point, I could see and feel the energy moving out in waves as if I were the pebble dropped into the lake. Something changed. I'm not sure what, but I was willing to let it go and wonder how it was going to show up in my life.

And that's where I began this letter. Today is only Thursday, and people are coming out of the woodwork calling me or stopping by to see if I want to go for a walk. I'm used to certain people calling, but these are all new people or ones who haven't contacted me in months, and in one case, a year and a half. Watching this unfold is so much fun—especially because I'm not holding onto a specific outcome. I wonder, what else will show up in my life? I wonder, what other habits are holding me back?

Habit Busting,

J

Note: This letter is long and rambling, but I kept it that way so you could see that you don't have to be perfect. Just get the ideas and emotions down on paper.

So, what actually happened?
How did this letter influence the outcome?

My husband and I have both dealt with the issue of not receiving whether it's not feeling worthy enough to receive, afraid someone will take advantage if we do receive, or something else. And things are turning around as we peel away the layers of resistance.

CHAPTER 33

PERFECTION

What Shows up Is Perfect ... On Some Level

It's all perfect. The concept of everything being perfect was a hard one for me. At first glance, it seems to say that things must *be* perfect. However, if you look at it as the collection of thoughts, feelings, actions, and activities that lead in a certain direction, then the conclusion of the things has led you to exactly where you are. This is perfect based on what has happened or what you've done.

For example, if your thoughts, feelings and actions led you to eat French fries all day every day, the result may be that you're overweight and sluggish. Based on what you did, you have the perfect outcome.

Using this principle, what you focus on—your thoughts, feelings, and actions—brings you to a perfect outcome for those thoughts, feelings, and actions. If you don't like what shows up, do something different. Simply change those thoughts, feelings, and actions.

Now don't get me wrong. I know that "perfection" and "everything is perfect" are two different things entirely. But once I opened to the idea that everything is perfect, life became easier. Easier to accept. Easier to live. Easier to be. It took the pressure off. And I know that at any point in time, I can make a different choice. I can change my thoughts, feelings, and actions. Isn't it great that we have so much influence over our own lives?

> Dear Future Lover,
>
> What does your "perfect" look like? If you could have a perfect life, what would that be? I wonder if our views of a perfect relationship and life are the same. What have you done to get to where you are? Are you striving for something more?
>
> Where are you now? I'm not talking about where are you physically. I'm asking about where are you on the inside and how has it shown up in your life.
>
> I guess, I'm also curious about whether we blend. Are you a banana and I'm an orange—and together we make a smoothie?
>
> I'm hungry for you...and I'm off to the refrigerator.
>
> Love,
> J

So, what actually happened?
How did this letter influence the outcome?

Our relationship is surprisingly drama-free. Neither of us likes to fight, so we don't. We have the ability to think similar thoughts and express them at the same time. It took a while to get to this point, and we had a lot of miscommunications, but now we laugh about how we talk differently. Most of the misunderstandings originate because he's from the South and I'm from the North. He says "stop street" and I say "stop sign." The more we are open to communicating more clearly, the easier our communications become.

CHAPTER 34

CREATE YOUR FUTURE

You Create Your Life

When you can create your future without reference to your past, you've moved to Level Three of Transformation. If you had no past, what would you create for your future? There would be nothing to hold you back or sway you one way or another. You would have total freedom to choose.

Imagine if you never had a bad relationship. You could choose whatever you'd like this new relationship to be. You could love freely. You could expect the best (and get it). You could have a great sex life without carrying the baggage of past relationships. You get to choose.

So why is this the last level and not the first? To be honest, the principles you learned—acceptance, non-judgment, intention, and others—while you were focusing on the problem and getting used to what "better" felt like will support your creations at this level. However, it *is* possible to jump to Level Three and start creating. It's just that most people are motivated to be, have, or do something different because of a problem, and they first desire to get rid of the problem. Then, they need time get used to feeling better to even believe it's possible. But what if you had no issues? What would your life be like?

Three Steps to Creating Your Future

It's time to jump into your life with a giant YES! and create your dreams, hopes, desires, and wishes. There are three steps at Level Three.

Step One: Imagine

Imagine your dream, hope, desire, or wish. Use any form you like…visualizing, journaling, listing, drawing, daydreaming, or something else. It doesn't matter as long as you can "see" your dreams. This is when you go into detail and explore your dream with all your senses.

Because I'm a writer, these letters helped me discover what I was dreaming about when I thought of my future husband—what he'd look like, what he was interested in, and so on. Often, I had no idea what I'd write until I wrote it. It's as if my subconscious was spilling out onto the page.

To do your dreaming, do what works for you. If you get stuck, ask yourself questions or have a friend ask you questions about your future dream.

Step Two: Feel

Feel the sensation you'll have in your body *when* you have your desire—in this case, when you're in a relationship with your future lover. In reality, while we think we want something (in this case a husband, wife, girlfriend, boyfriend, or someone else), what we're truly going for are sensations or feelings we'll have once we have him or her. This is why it's important to know what you're striving for regarding feelings.

Focus on the feeling by feeding it. Do things that will help the feeling grow within you. The more you *feed* it, the more you *feel* it, and the more things you'll have in your life to give you this feeling.

This way, no matter what happens, you'll have the feeling, and the desire will become one way to feel it, not the only way.

The same theory works here as with gratitude. If you feel it before you have it, you become a magnet, pulling your desired feelings to you. It may show up differently from what you imagined, but it *will* show up. The important thing is to actually feel the sensation as much as possible—not just label it.

Remember, when you raise your vibration, you'll bring more ease into your life all around and not just with this dream, hope, wish, or desire. (Ways to raise your vibration are scattered throughout this book. More are included in the next few chapters.) Your vibration will influence the quality of everything in your life and your reaction to those things. The closer you are to peace, joy, gratitude, and kindness, the less "efforting" will be required and the more clearly you will be able to feel your desired feelings.

Step Three: Do Inspired Actions

This is when you actually *do* something and take an action. But it's not just any action. It's an *inspired* action. It won't necessarily look like what others would do. It may be "out of order," and it may not make sense in the moment. But do it anyway.

An inspired action is something that pops up in your consciousness as the next tiny step you can take. It's a thought that feels very strong. The Universe is leading you to prepare for the arrival of the desire. Trust what shows up.

Dear Future Lover,

If I hadn't been married before—heck, if I never dated before—what would I choose our relationship to be? When I considered this, the first feeling that popped up was fear. I'd probably be overwhelmed by the choices or not have the confidence earned by years of experience. But that quickly cleared.

So, what would I desire? Since I love research, I'd probably ask what other people would like. I'd check out my romance books and see what sounded feasible. I might even read some relationship books.

But in the end, I'd probably come to smooth sailing. As I sit here looking out at the lake, a sailboat passed by. Yes, I'd choose smooth sailing...with the thrill of the full sails and the wind rushing in our faces (with huge smiles, of course). Perhaps there would be waves along the way to make things even more interesting. We'd be in sync, working together toward a common goal.

What would that goal be? Having fun and enjoying our lives.

This sounds like something I'd like.

And look—I didn't even need to research anything. I'm just picturing us sailing together and feeling the excitement in my chest as we are fully engaged in our lives.

Yes. This is it.

Sending love,

J

So, what actually happened?
How did this letter influence the outcome?

While we've never sailed together, Bruce is a fisherman and has owned many boats. He prefers speedboats over sailboats. It makes sense that he likes speed—after all, he was a sprint car driver.

An old memory just surfaced. Years ago, I was sailing with my parents and their friends. I was feeling snarky (as do many teenagers) and I remember muttering, "Are we having fun yet?" Perhaps it's the knowing that I really shouldn't have said that out loud that caused it to stick in my mind. That being said, as an adult, I can see the value of sailing—as well as speedboats. Fun is in my *attitude*, not the thing I'm doing.

In other ways, Bruce has helped me push beyond my hesitation, and I'm more willing to fully engage in life. I have a sneaking suspicion that the more I engage in life, the lighter I'll feel and the better our relationship will become.

By the way, with Bruce as a fun coach, sex has also become more fun and includes more laughter!

Chapter 35

YES!

Take Charge of Your Life. Say YES!

You are your hero, so quit wasting time pretending you can't do something. Are you telling yourself that all the great lovers are taken and the only ones left are the bottom of the barrel? Is this the rule you've chosen to believe and live your life by? If so, *that is exactly what you will find.*

But here's a truth: You only need one lover. So, it doesn't really matter how many inadequate ones are out there. In fact, if you focus on yourself and say YES! with joy, you'll attract other people who vibrate at your level, and you'll find your match.

You get to decide what you'd like to be, have, and do. Jump into your life with a giant YES! If you're serious about saying YES! with joy, you'll find a way.

What will it take? Begin by looking at everything that's wrong—but that's for Levels One and Two. For Level Three, find the *gold* in your life. When something happens, look for the gold. Look for what is right about something that is supposedly bad.

Remember the fall in the bathroom that I mentioned in the chapter on signs (Chapter 28). I knew something positive would come from it. As it turns out, my knee now moves with more ease. I'd been dealing with a funky knee for a year before that fall. It had improved, but I still couldn't sit comfortably on the floor with my legs crossed. After a few trips to a chiropractor, I sat down to meditate and automatically crossed my legs. It took a few minutes to dawn on me! In addition, my chiropractor said that my body was moving differently. I call this a win. My knee had been "stuck," and the Universe gave me a way to unstick it.

So where are you stuck? This "stuckness" shows up for many people when they're afraid to finish something because it's not perfect yet. That's what *versions* are for. Finish version one, get it out there, and then start working on version two. Take it one step at a time, but take the step.

For example, when I wrote the first draft of this book, I dragged my fingers, and it took over a year. But I did it. As I finished it, I realized that it should be organized differently. It took only three months to complete version two, and this included time off for my birthday weekend, family stuff, and my husband's knee replacement, when I played concerned wife and nurse. After an additional tweaking or two, it was out of my hands.

The same is true of your online profile, if you have one of those. Put something on the profile. Get it out there, and then tweak it as necessary.

Finally, quit wasting your time. If it's not flowing for you, do something else and then come back. Play, then create. Or create, then play. Or switch it up depending on the day. However, if you're getting lost in the something else, you might evaluate whether the thing you desire to do is *truly* your desire. Does it light you up? If not, how could it be tweaked so it does?

Do you truly want a future lover? Or is your mother, father, best friend, officemate (or anyone else) pushing the idea on you? Look at what you truly would like. What do you dream of? When you discover this and align with your desire, the task won't seem so daunting.

Here's a clue to give you the YES! that will help you accomplish your desire: Get your vibration as high as you can. This way, you'll invite ease into the activity. Raising your vibration can be done before or after you imagine your desire. Play with what works for you.

When I write, I like to listen to baroque music. It helps me move forward at a nice pace. (But first, I've meditated, exercised, done some neutralizing/releasing, and maybe even had some intimate time with my hubby.)

Here is an exercise to help you narrow down your dreams, hopes, desires, and wishes. Write your eulogy. That's right—pretend you've lived 100 years and write about yourself from someone else's point of view. This person is telling the world what a wonderful person you were. Include things you did in your life, differences you made in the world, and people you touched. When you look this over, you'll see that these are your desires. This is who you would like to be.

Now, what would it take to get there? That's up to you. After all, you're in charge of your life. *You get to decide.*

Dear Future Lover,

I'm so excited. I know you're almost here. I can feel it. I have butterflies in my chest. Logically, I know that I can release this feeling, but honestly, I sort of like it. I think I'll hold onto it for a while longer.

When are we going to meet in the flesh? We have already met in the ethers. Our higher selves have already been busy rearranging things in both of our lives. How much more has to be rearranged before we can meet?

> I asked the Universe, "What needs to happen on my end to help this along?" I heard, "Make a decision!" I wonder what I have to make a decision about? I'm sure it will show up. I'm willing to release anything that gets in my way of knowing and perceiving everything I can do or be to help the situation along.
>
> I'm anxious and excited to meet you. It's going to be so much fun.
>
> Waiting excitedly,
>
> J

So, what actually happened?
How did this letter influence the outcome?

At the time of our meeting, my energy was on its way up. It wasn't as high as it is now, but I was moving higher from the lower vibrations. I was on a cruise—actually, it was two cruises, back to back. At the end of the first cruise, I spoke with Dr. Jahner and another friend. They cornered me and asked *if I wanted to live*. I hadn't even known this was an issue! We did some releasing and then I decided YES!

At this point, Bruce booked a stateroom. He hadn't been able to get on the first cruise, but he stayed in Miami just in case he could get on the second. It's a good thing he did. We met within the first hour of the second cruise…after I'd made the decision to grab life and live.

And as for Bruce clearing up his life for me, he was going through a party phase and had to complete this before we met, since I'm not much of a partier.

CHAPTER 36

COHERENCE

Flow with the River

Life is easier when things are in flow and moving in the same direction. It's like floating in a river. If you go with the flow, you're coherent with it. If you swim against the flow, you're incoherent.

The same thing happens in your body. When you're coherent, you're healthy and your body is working as a unified whole with all available possibilities. On the other hand, when you're incoherent, you're more likely to be ill. The less coherent you are, the more mixed up and confused your body is, limiting your possibilities.

Think of coherence as happy, happy, happy, and even more happy. (Interestingly, sad, sad, sad, sad is still coherent in a way, but you won't have a lot of energy to create.) Whereas, incoherence is happy, sad, happy, sad, happy, sad, happy, sad, and so on. The more coherent you are, the less confused your energy will be.

So, what does this mean for creating your future? The higher vibrations are more coherent, and the more time you spend feeling them, the more coherent you'll be. Life will have even more ease.

If you want to make things harder, that's also possible. You can talk about love, but then remember and feel every other time you've been cheated on when a past lover professed to love you but didn't act that way, or you never actually give thanks for the love that is coming or is already there in your life.

To create your future lover, get everything moving in the same direction…thoughts, feelings, and actions. For example, if you're thinking about the love you'll have, take the time to feel it now and take some action, such as writing in your journal. Pretend you have the love now. Give thanks for it and allow it to show up in many areas of your life. It's that simple.

Coherence is needed to create with ease. Remember floating in the river? That's going with the flow. That's ease. The higher your vibe, the more coherent your energy.

Dear Future Lover,

The space between our bodies, our touch, is too great. I miss the feeling of your skin against mine. Your hand in mine. Your arm around me. The touch of our lips as we come together softly. Even the thought of this kiss leaves me panting with desire. My breath becomes shallow as I feel your lips as they will be and I sigh.

Then my mind wanders, running away from desire, from what I don't have in this moment. It's a trick I learned—to turn off my desire so I'm not left wanting.

Will you be the one to turn on this desire? Can you find my "on" switch? Or do I have to turn it on and then find you?

Getting my thoughts in line are the first steps to attracting you. As I sleep tonight, I'll be dreaming of you in my life. The dreams will be so sweet.

Good night my love,
J

Judith Joy

So, what actually happened?
How did this letter influence the outcome?

The more Bruce and I are together, the more coherent we become in our relationship. It's reached the point that if one of us says something, the other says, "I was just thinking that." It gives us lots of laughs.

CHAPTER 37

AWARENESS

There Is Nothing You Need to Be or Do to Be Who You Are.

If all the limitations we collect over a lifetime are dirt, we still exist under that dirt. Our biggest limitation is that we're in the habit of thinking that there are limitations and forgetting that it's just *us* under the dirt. We assign meaning to the filth and grime and are so busy looking at it that we don't see *us*.

Awareness is like this. It's perceiving and knowing the difference between the dirt and you. Awareness brings clarity.

Wouldn't you love to have a lover who accepts you for you? Wouldn't it be easier to be you if you knew who you were? That's what consciousness transformation is about—discovering who you are without the limitations. The more consciousness transformation you experience, the more awareness you will have.

What does this mean? Again, the more you operate at the higher vibrations, the more you will be able to perceive and know without past limitations. At the higher vibrations, it's easier to see you and not the dirt.

The more you discover who you are, the higher your vibration is. Here's a clue: The higher your vibration is, the easier it is to discover who you are. It's as if the higher vibration washes away the dirt.

Why does this apply to creating your future lover? The more you know who you are and the higher you vibrate, the more chance you have of attracting someone who is also of a higher vibration. Remember, like attracts like. If you're an angry person, then you'll attract someone who resonates with anger.

Let's say your last relationship didn't end well. In truth, the whole relationship was filled with fighting, screaming, and anger. You're finally out of that relationship. But if you don't raise your vibration, you will be the same and will attract someone else with the same vibration. You will attract a similar person (with a similar vibration). He will just have a different body. New person. New body. Old vibe.

The higher your vibration climbs, the more aware you'll be and the easier it will be to have a sense of knowing and perceiving so you can see things more clearly. When you *do* see things clearly, the awareness will feel expansive instead of contracted.

Catch yourself when you say: "I notice," "I figured it out," "I just became aware of," "Oh, I get it," or "I know…" These are signs that you have an awareness. Check in with your gut. If your gut feels contracted or the awareness feels heavy, something isn't working for you. If your whole being lights up and you feel expansive, something about the awareness *does* work for you.

You'll be able to see that the guy you thought was so great (because he felt familiar and comfortable) treated the waitress very poorly. You'll have a sense of awareness that you don't choose to be treated that way, and thus can make a choice not to continue to date that guy. If you didn't have the awareness, the fact that he "felt comfortable" doing that would send you down a different path.

The more you clean up your consciousness, the more you'll be able to see who you truly are and the more awareness you'll have, which leads to making choices that work for you.

Dear Future Lover,

Power isn't a drug. It's more of confidence—at least true personal power is. A king may have power, but still be affected by insecurities. But the true power from within is just a knowing. This is confidence.

Amazingly, this is how I feel after my Level 4 Matrix Energetics* workshop. At times it was confusing and overwhelming but, by the end, it all came together in my being. I feel confident. I know I can make a difference. Somewhere along the way, standing in the shadows of effectiveness, uncertainty fell away. I am effective—just what my intention was for the weekend—to be or increase my effectiveness by 10x or more.

On the second day, I knew my intention was to absorb the information and be able to use it as needed. It wasn't to memorize and remember. Very different intentions. As a result, my body has a very different feeling around the intention. The absorbing and using was comforting. I felt in resonance with it. I felt congruent.

I've noticed this a lot about setting an intention. It's a calming feeling when I'm in resonance. However, this connection happens only if the intention reflects the true wish or desire. It's important to look underneath for what is really wanted. After all, you may be limiting the possibilities if you don't.

Let's take my intention to go to a party and have fun. Already, that causes my chest and throat to close up and flutter. Let's look further within. What do I really want? Connection and company. Below that? Acceptance. Below that? Feeling worthwhile. Below that? A reason to live. Below that? A sense of excitement. Below that? The word "basking" comes up. I don't know what it means, but I'm going to go with it. Each time I asked, "below that?" and an answer appeared, another level of calm settled in my chest.

So, what might the intention show up as? To feel accepted and worthwhile while basking in excitement? Or to bask in the excitement of living? The second one is more positive and feels uplifting. It's almost as if a part of me says, "Yeah. That's it." By the way, trust what shows up. That's very important!

Now that the intention is chosen (to bask in the excitement of living) you can see how going to the party is one way of doing it, but it may show up in a dozen or a hundred different ways. If you stopped at the party intention, you'd be missing all the other opportunities because you don't even know that's what you really want. The opportunities will be there, but you probably won't recognize them.

Let's say that on the way to the party, something exciting happens that fills your heart and raised your vibration. It could be something small—a stranger hands you a flower as you walk by. The feeling of receiving may trigger you to help the next person who needs your assistance, even if it's only offering a smile. Here, you've found the feeling of your intention perhaps even recognized it.

Or the opportunity that showed up was a friend calling to ask you to go sailing. But if the intention was just to go to the party, which is supposed to be fun, but you never quite find parties fun, so by going to the party, the other opportunities might not be recognized. And if you don't go to the party, you'll feel like you've failed, even if you took advantage of the other opportunities.

You know where I'm going with all this—dig deep, be open, accept what shows up. Of course, if you don't like what shows up, go back to your intention and redo it.

Now, dear, all you have to do is change all those you's to I's and you'll have a window into my soul.

Once I've chosen the intention, I can matrix it and remove any blockages that might be in the way. The matrix will help even more opportunities that work for you will appear, because I'll be more in resonance with what I really want.

These thoughts have been swirling around in my head, and today I had the confidence to write them down. Plus, I had the added benefit to rephrase this intention. Previously, it was to have a passion that I could be absorbed in. This never felt right. Now, to bask in the excitement of living—that feels expansive! But in my usual way, I start dissecting and wonder if bask is the best word. For today it is. For me to bask also means to feel, but it's the type of feeling with my face turned up toward the sun and a deep sigh in my chest. It feels like I'm going to open my eyes and see the fairies and angels.

Are you one of those angels? Will I see you soon? Have I already?

Waiting excitedly,

J

*Matrix Energetics is a consciousness transformation program that I love. It's fun, easy and creates great results. At the time I wrote this journal, I'd just gone to another Matrix Energetics seminar and was focused on learning that.

So, what actually happened?
How did this letter influence the outcome?

My husband is my angel, my cheerleader, my lover, my friend, and so much more. As my fun coach, he is teaching me about basking in the excitement of living. Since meeting him, I have traveled to the Philippines, Honduras and Europe, gone to several sprint car races, wintered in Florida, written two books, started teaching again, and have even more confidence in my abilities. And it all feels great.

Chapter 38

IMAGINE

All of Life Is Made up. Imagine Your Future.

All of life is just something that people have imagined already. The house you live in was first imagined by someone. As was the car, bus or train you ride. As was the job you do. And, yes, even the books you read. Someone imagined the possibility before it became a reality.

So, what would it take to use this to your advantage? Make the assumption that what you imagine can be your future. (After all, it is anyway.) It can work for you, and it's easy. All you have to do is imagine your dreams, hopes, wishes, and desires as if they were real and already here. Feeding the feeling will power the assumption.

This is where you fantasize about your dreams, hopes, wishes, and desires. Expand your fantasy. Ask, "What if reality is better than my fantasy?"

To start with ask, "What might I like?" and then be curious about it. Let your mind wander until you get the expansive feeling that lets you know you're moving in a direction that will benefit you.

As the imaginer of your dreams, you get to be curious and ask yourself questions. You get to look at everything with wonder. You're the magician who will create the final scene.

At the end of the movie *Sleepless in Seattle*, Sam and Annie look at each other as they get into the elevator, and they smile shyly as their happiness expands. The rest of the movie is just a way to get to this point.

Everything that leads up to the final scene is the *how*. Imagine your final scene and don't worry at all about how it's done! Just keep an open mind and compare every thought, action, and feeling to your final scene and what that will feel like. Will that thought, feeling or action help you get to the final scene? How can it be even more useful than you could have imagined?

Every feeling, action, word, and thought (spoken, written, or just floating through your head) has the ability to magnetize and attract exactly what you're asking for. However, very often the essence of what you are asking for will be what is attracted and will appear in some way that you never imagined.

Be aware of what you ask for or expect. By the time I wrote my journal, I understood how important it was to write from the final scene, but I forgot. In the following letter, I wasn't careful with my words, and I wrote that I was looking for someone motivated to succeed. I realized that being motivated to be successful isn't the same as actually *being successful*. This is a slight difference, but an important one.

So, when you ask for something, be aware of *what* you are asking for. Look at it from all sides and consider how your request might show up. Then refine your wording and the picture it paints. See it as if you're looking through your eyes instead of from the perspective of being in an audience watching a movie. After all, it's you in your future.

Dear Future Lover,

Who are you? What have I ordered from the Universe? At one time, I wrote pages of what I was looking for in a man—including the button-down shirt. After all, if I didn't place the order, I could get just anything, which most certainly isn't what I want.

But now, as I pare down the list, I think the latest version is you. Someone who is kind, easy to look at, motivated to succeed, generous, and interested in me—all of me.

Most everything fits within these. Kindness covers a lot of traits—faithfulness, honesty, and trustworthiness. A person who is truly kind is concerned about others and peaceful in his approach to life. Kindness is such a gentle word. I think you'll be gentle also. Don't get me wrong—I'm not looking for a wimp. But I do know that you are kind to all—including yourself.

My grandma knew that Papa Jerry was the man for her partly because he was so kind and considerate to his sister. How you treat others is a barometer of how you'll treat me.

As for the other qualities, they're pretty self-explanatory, although I'd like to clarify the success one. "Motivated to succeed" seems to be an appropriate way to phrase it, since the motivation and drive are what I'm really after. Success itself can come in many forms, of which money is only one. (Now, if you happen to have money, that's great.) But I don't want to limit you. If you're a teacher and are working hard helping kids learn, that's success too. I'm looking for a man who is motivated and successful, however that is defined.

Love,

J

So, what actually happened?
How did this letter influence the outcome?

My husband was very successful as a chiropractor, but is retired. Currently, he is launching another career with his patented formulations.

CHAPTER 39

RELATIONSHIP

Balance the Relationship to Neutrality

Everything is in a relationship with something or someone else. People, things, sensations, thoughts, and more. Me to myself. You to yourself. You to me. Where you are to where you'd like to be. Your point of view to another point of view. You to the chair you're sitting in as you read this book. The chair to your body. You're in a relationship to this book and the book is in relationship to you. You get the idea.

The goal is to recognize the relationship and neutralize it so any sensations that have a hold on you can be released. (This can be done in a variety of ways, listed throughout the book.) The important thing is to recognize the relationship, make a choice about it, and release anywhere that it's stuck to you. This allows more possibilities to appear.

For example, let's talk about sex…the-hot-and-sweaty, heart-pumping, can't-get-enough kind. Quick check: what are you feeling right now? You might feel uncomfortable or even excited about what might be coming next. You might feel a flutter in your chest. You might have judged me because I may be writing about sex.

Now, what if I'm writing about connections, and I never mention the word "sex"? What do you feel now? Disappointment? Relief? Confusion?

Whatever you felt was actually a sensation that was sticking you, possibly causing you to have an emotional hiccup. The feeling was fast and brief, but it was still there. When you notice these feelings, your body is telling you that you have a point of view. It's okay to have a point of view, but isn't it more useful to be open to a *new* point of view and not be stuck in cement?

When you're neutral, you can be an observer and see everything as interesting. Nothing is holding you back. You're not holding onto one point of view as if it's the only one out there. This is when ease happens. This is when what you're asking for "walks right up to your front door" and into your awareness. You still have to take the action of opening the door.

Possibilities appear more quickly and without requiring you to spin your wheels so much. You can actually *see* the possibilities when they do appear. You don't push them away because of the points of view you were holding onto.

Hand Balancing

Here's a releasing/neutralizing exercise that will help you balance two sides of any relationship. It's one of my favorite methods—hand balancing.

Put both your hands in front of you, elbows at your side, palms up. In one hand, place an imaginary something—a thought, color, item, anything. In the other hand, place a different imaginary something. These two "things" are now in a relationship.

Which hand feels heavier?

Now, pour the heavier feeling into the other hand. Mix it with the feeling in that hand. Then, pour that feeling into the first hand. Repeat. Repeat. Repeat. Stop when the hands feel equal. This is when the relationship is neutralized. I usually get a sigh or an expansive feeling when this happens.

The first time I tried this, it took 45 minutes to feel the change in energy. Now it takes about two seconds. I had to learn to feel the sensations in my body and then be willing to allow them to be different.

Try the following match-ups. Place one in each hand and start to balance until the pairing is neutralized. (Some match-ups may not feel different. This just means that they're already neutralized. Go on to the next pairing.)

- ♥ Your past relationships—Your new relationship
- ♥ Rejecting your past—Accepting your future
- ♥ Rejecting yourself—Accepting yourself
- ♥ Accepting someone into your life—Keeping others away
- ♥ Your ideal book boyfriend—The guys you would never like to have a relationship with
- ♥ Afraid of the future—Afraid of the past
- ♥ Rose color—Green color
- ♥ Loving all of you—Being effervescent
- ♥ Loving all of you—Allowing others to love you
- ♥ Loving all of you—Allowing others to love you even more than you love yourself
- ♥ Accepting your power—Stepping into your power
- ♥ Finding your lover—Never finding your lover
- ♥ You loving your lover—Your lover loving you
- ♥ Being married—Never being married
- ♥ Your lover has blond hair –Your lover has brown hair
- ♥ You know how you'll meet him—You have no clue as to how you'll meet him
- ♥ Being intimate together—Being vulnerable

- ♥ Vulnerability—Safety
- ♥ You contribute to the relationship—He contributes to the relationship
- ♥ You get to do what you like—He gets to do what he likes
- ♥ Great relationship—Fantastic relationship
- ♥ Living together—Living together in peace and harmony

You may notice that some interesting pairings are going on. Some are opposites. Some don't seem to be connected at all. Others are a choice paired with a more expansive choice. And if you think of other pairings, great. Go with those.

Remember—*what you focus on is what you get*. While it's beneficial to dig a bit into the not-haves, it's actually more powerful to focus on the possibilities than the problems.

Dear Future Lover,

Going to bed has been feeling weird. The room is too quiet. My mind isn't turning off. My body feels as if it's only half there. This is a strange feeling, almost as if I'm too light or even empty. I lie on my side "facing you" and the sinking-into-the-bed feeling just isn't there. I'm having thoughts about sex. I feel as if I'm missing a part of me that can only be filled with you. It's more than sex—it's a true energetic connection.

I guess this whole thing isn't about unfolding but about making connections-- physical, emotional, or psychic.

Connections exist all around us. Unfortunately, many times we miss the thin threads bringing them together. I always find it so interesting when I read something totally unrelated and a connection jumps off the page.

For example, now that I'm writing to you, my love, (whoops, did an endearment just slip out?) ideas are leaping out at me no matter what I'm doing. I had a fleeting thought that maybe I should bring my good camera to San Francisco tomorrow. I usually don't travel with it, but the thought was there. Just a few hours later, Shoshi called and mentioned that her friend in San Francisco (whom I will be visiting) is a photographer. Who knows where this will lead? Maybe it will just be fun. Maybe it's a new way to see the city. Shoshi just called—her friend said, "Bring your camera." This is going to be fun.

Choosing love,

J

So, what actually happened?
How did this letter influence the outcome?

We have talked every day since we met. The connections are getting stronger and stronger. After a few years, we can more easily see where we aren't neutral and then shift to a neutral feeling. This improves our communications and our relationship.

Chapter 40

ACCEPTANCE AND ALLOWANCE

"Should-bust" Your Way to a Higher Vibration

Are you seeing a recurring theme in Level Three? Raise your vibration! Life is so much easier if you quit judging everything, worrying about if it's right and wrong. This drags you down and lowers your vibration. Learn not to be pulled into the void of ever-increasing "holding onto the way you think it should be." Things just *are*. Accept it and allow it to be what it is…until you create something else. Do what you choose, by raising your vibration. Then, you can create the future lover of your dreams.

If you can look at the guy across the table from you as he chews with his mouth open and just accept him for who he is and allow him to be himself, you'll be happier, which raises your vibration. From that point of acceptance and allowance, you're then free to choose to keep talking, leave, laugh, or do something else entirely. But during the whole process, you're at ease.

From this place, things just become interesting. And when things are interesting, it's much easier to let go of conclusions, which limit the possibilities, and you can then step into the wave of infinite possibilities.

Acceptance and allowance are "should-busters." So, the next time you have a strong feeling about something, try to just accept it and allow it to be whatever it is. Then, think, "That's interesting. I wonder what else can I choose or create?"

In the process, you'll raise your vibration. Without an attachment or resistance to things going the way you think or feel it should go, you're free to look at the world as entertainment.

Dear Future Lover,

So many exciting things are happening with the matrix.

At Adam's wrestling meet, I was flipping energy. No particular intention to win, but I wasn't going to turn that down either. I was just helping them to do their best. Well, they did. Adam even came over to me and said, "Did you see how great we're doing?" I told him I was flipping energy for the team, and he asked me to keep doing it.

When I asked if there was anyone special I should be matrixing, he said, "Mitch." So, in the second set of matches, I played with Mitch's energy. First, I closed my eyes, then I tried watching. I had to close them again to maintain my calm. I could feel all the anxiety when my eyes were open. During the third period, I looked up at the ceiling and saw nails sticking down. My thoughts went to swords in the back. I removed the swords from Mitch's back, and he pinned his opponent. Yahoo!

As for Adam, the opposing teams didn't have wrestlers at 103 pounds. So, Adam agreed to wrestle up, and faced a 119-pounder. He pinned the guy in 30 seconds. He's so much better than he was last year. Yippee!

Now for the really cool thing. A mother tripped on the corner of the mat, face-planted on the gym floor, and was knocked out. (That isn't the cool part.) Someone called an ambulance, but before it got there, I started playing with her energy. (This is the cool part.) She awoke and sat up. From across the gym, I "heard" her say that her knee and back hurt, so I continued flipping energy until she got up and walked away. I "heard" that she told the EMTs she was fine and didn't need their help. It was as if I heard her in my mind. Very cool.

I'm glad I was able to help her—and all from across the gym—without having any intention other than sending her love.

While flipping energy, something wild happened. I noticed that she was in focus and everything else in the room was out of focus. Also, I felt very strong energy changes instead of the usual softer ones. When I asked Jahner, he said it was awesome.—that the blurring is energy so strong it intensifies the aura and shifts dimensional reality.

Jahner and I have had three great sessions in the last six weeks or so. Each time he says I'm more powerful than ever before (doing Matrix Energetics) and do more work in a session then all the previous years combined. He says there is a huge shift coming and he predicts it will shift within the next three months... in time for the next Matrix seminar at the end of February.

As for my energy shift, I was feeling comfortable loving myself. This showed up with lots of effusive compliments over the weekend. I didn't know what to say other than "thank you."

Today, I matrixed Sandy and Shay and we focused on being happy and having wealth. Later in the day, I found a penny on the sidewalk. I'm glad I have the rule that every session I do for others helps me also. I'm now a penny richer.

But enough for now. It's time for my bath and then bed.

Love you tons,

J

So, what actually happened?
How did this letter influence the outcome?

When my husband and I first got together, I was excited to show him about Matrix Energetics. I did a little bit of flipping energy and asked him if he could feel it. He said, "Yes. And I can see it." We both laughed. He'd been using it in his chiropractic practice and hadn't been aware of it. He used it in the physical, while I use it to change more than the physical.

CHAPTER 41

OBSERVE

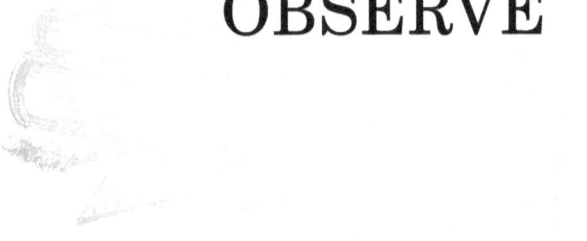

Zip It, Watch, and Listen

To observe is to take in information by noticing and perceiving. This doesn't mean to talk (even in your own head), give your opinion, or judge, but it does leave room to ask questions. When you take yourself out of the equation, what else is left?

Most people can converse, although their version is to latch onto something the other person has said and then think or talk about how they are the same and have had a similar experience, and then talk about the experience. It's normal to want to find a connection point and feel that you can identify with the other person.

Then there are those people who look for something to argue about. The end result is that the "listener" must find a place to jump into the conversation.

What happens if you don't do this? You can observe what is actually there and what is truly happening or being said. Notice *what is there*, not *what you think should be there*.

This takes a lot of weight off your shoulders. Imagine listening to a conversation and not being worried about contributing. Or sitting across from someone and perceiving what they *mean*, not just what they *say*. You don't have to jump in. You don't have to do anything other than notice and perceive in a nonjudgmental way. From this point, you can make a choice. And as an added bonus, you'll feel more self-compassion and kindness because you are more relaxed within yourself.

On one date, I sat across from a man who told me that what I believed wasn't that simple. According to him, life is more multi-layered. I sat back and observed. From his viewpoint (and his outer appearance) he was right. He wore a sweater vest, a corduroy jacket with patches on the elbows, a big coat, hat, scarf, and gloves. He literally *wore* his belief that life was multi-layered!

An interesting thing happens when you observe—your intuition sharpens. You're able to know and perceive more. The more you observe, the more you see.

Recently, after an intense few sessions of observing more within me, I was waiting for the yoga room to open up. I looked up. There were two giant (and I mean giant) pictures above the racks that held items for sale. I'd never noticed them before. But now I did. I wonder what else I haven't seen when I thought my eyes were open?

What will you do with your sharpened intuition? Use it to help you weed out the duds. Whether those duds are future lovers, jobs, or even a TV show, the stronger your intuition becomes, the more you'll be able to feel, trust, and follow it… straight to a more expansive life that works for you.

And this is done by zipping your lips, clearing your mind, and observing. This is pretty amazing stuff.

Dear Future Lover,

It's Thanksgiving and the troops have descended on us. Family and family of family came from across the country this year. It was a great weekend...especially with a new engagement.

I want to tell you about the "session" I had with some of the adults. They were interested in what I do, and the best way to help them understand was to do a session. So, Saturday afternoon, while the "kids" were out and about, we sat in the living room and talked.

"A" wants to get married. But I realized she doesn't want to marry her boyfriend of 12 years. She told me later that her eyes were now opened. During the session, she said she felt energy throughout her body. Her knees were wobbly, and then she fell backward onto the couch.

"B" was quiet during the session. I whispered to him when I picked up on his hidden anxiety. He never told me of an intention to shift. He only thought of it. I told him he'd be able to pay for his daughter's wedding and that he can get off the merry-go-round chasing money. He smiled. He hasn't shared anything with me since then about what's different.

"C" protested that she was happy with her "box" and didn't want me to work on her. As the group conversed, she mentioned that she wants to lose weight. So, I started quietly flipping energy to allow for her possibility. She wasn't aware of it until I told her two days later. Then today, she e-mailed me that something is working as she isn't craving sweets. Great! (I offered the energy shifts as a gift. It's up to her if she wanted to accept them.)

Thankfully yours,

J

So, what actually happened?
How did this letter influence the outcome?

My husband observes on a physical level since he's a chiropractor, and he's very skilled at it. In the metaphysical world (the deeper meaning beyond the obvious) he still draws conclusions from what he's observing. The problem comes in when he assumes that the conclusion is correct instead of just noticing and perceiving what is there to be seen or heard, but he's improving. (And very wisely, if I gain weight, he doesn't say anything. ☺)

CHAPTER 42

THE ENERGY YOU *BE* IS VITAL

Be to Become

Before writing this chapter, my husband and I had the most amazing energy session. He had a big meeting scheduled for the next day, and I asked him if I could facilitate a session with him. He was on board with it. Up until then, he'd done it reluctantly, but this time it was amazing for both of us. And his desires came true for the meeting.

What made it amazing? My energy was high—very high. I'd had a great day with a lot of releasing, two fantastic client sessions, some great insights, reading on the beach, a few YouTube videos and more. I was so happy, I was giddy. From this giddy high, it was easy to shift the energy. It was the energy that I was *being* that made the difference. We both felt the waves of change. Amazing!

Think about that the next time you do something. If you're dreading it and see it as a "have to" or "should," shift your energy to a higher vibration.

This became clear to me while talking to a fellow author. He wondered about my process. Did I set a specific time every day to write? A certain number of words? He wanted to know what my structure was.

I think I blew his mind when I said that I don't write unless I feel the tingling sensation as if it's about to explode out of me. But then I followed it up with this: If I don't feel that way, I shift my energy and feelings until the words are bursting to come out.

The feelings come first.

The same is true with anything you'd like to draw in from the future to the now. The higher your vibe, the easier it is to do this. Anything you can do to boost your energy will bring more ease into your life. Keep reaching for the higher vibe.

How much effort is required to create a change? The energy you are is what you have to work with…until you change your vibration. If you have a low vibration (such as depression), it takes a lot of effort to create anything. As you increase your vibration (possibly to anger), it will take less effort to create your desires. Keep moving up the scale to joy, kindness, peace, calm, and love, and things happen effortlessly.

Obviously, wherever you are is the energy that powers your life. From this place, you influence the outcome. It is *the energy you're being* that will give you power to create your desires. In other words, be to become. Be the energy you hope to be *before* you have whatever you desire to become, have, or do.

It's best to boost your vibration to the highest level possible to give yourself the power of ease. You can analyze your thoughts and feelings, or you can choose to just *be* the energy you desire to become.

Boost Your Vibration with These "Love Moments:"

- ♥ <u>Imagine expanding your energy.</u> Breathe in and out slowly as your energy expands to the ends of the world and beyond. Feel your jaw relax. Feel your shoulders lower. Do this whenever you have a few minutes - for

- ♥ example, when you wake up, drift off to sleep, wait at a stoplight, or stand in line at the grocery store. Repeat it throughout the day.
- ♥ <u>Focus within your heart.</u> Feel the love building within you as if you're snuggling a baby. Or imagine giving love to a baby, the homeless guy on the street, a tree, your bedroom, anything or anyone. You can do something concrete, or you can use an imaginary "magic wand" to direct your love at the person or item. It doesn't matter who or what you're giving love to. What matters is that you *feel* it.
- ♥ <u>Pretend you're taking a shower of love.</u> Stand with your face tilted upwards and imagine love pouring on you. Feel the tension slip off you and down the drain. Stay with the imagination until you feel calm and expansive and you can feel your heart turn on.

The idea is to be the energy vibration so that you can become, have or do your desires, dreams, hopes, and wishes. The higher vibe you are, the less effort it will take to create these things.

Dear Future Lover,

An energetic high feels so sparkly. I've been processing a lot since the Matrix seminar. But today topped it all. My intention was "to allow change." Boy, did stuff happen! I did Matrix three separate times and also while driving to and from acupuncture.

Later, I had lunch with Shay and her business director, Sandy. I said that I'd like to support Integrative Touch for Kids, Shay's organization. I'd like to be a practitioner at their next summer retreat, and I'd like to do Matrix on their business for no charge. In exchange, I asked for a referral letter. I joked about wanting it only if good stuff happens, which I know it will. I felt confident in asking or saying what I wanted. And they were thrilled!

Dr. Jahner says I'm on the brink of my greatness. He may be right. It's all so exciting!

Paul, a client, called tonight and said that, since our last session, business has really picked up, and he's working very hard. He wants to tell me more.

This idea of working on businesses through their owners may be something great. It certainly feels right. More than right—it feels solid.

Tonight, for the first time, it also feels solid that I can be happy whether others are or aren't. Then we threw beautiful in there too. The shifting was easy. Jahner pointed me in the direction, and I did the shifting. By the time we were done, I was smiling and silly. It even felt like my body was as fluid as if I'd been drinking.

Now, I just have to get used to the new me. It will be fun. I hope that you're also on this path of change. It will be a fun ride together if we can keep the same (or close to the same) pace.

Love,

J

So, what actually happened?
How did this letter influence the outcome?

My husband wasn't on this path at the beginning, but he sees the value of it the more I flipped energy…and now he is starting to do it also.

CHAPTER 43

BOOST YOUR VIBRATION

Be the True You

This is simple—do whatever you can to get your vibration as high as possible. After all, the true you is a high-vibrational being. We have just covered our true self with lots of "dirt," some of which we were born with and some that we picked up along the way.

Most people move only slightly from the set point at which they're born. However, if you desire a different life, a life that works for you, you'll need to raise your vibration and hold it as high as possible for as long as possible.

This is done through shedding what doesn't work and becoming familiar with the higher vibrations. Is the transition comfortable? Probably not. But then, whenever you learn something new, you experience growing pains. Just because it's uncomfortable doesn't mean it's *wrong*. It's just new.

And because a higher vibration is new, it will take some time to get used to. But the more you are at the higher vibrations, the more at ease you will be with them.

So, let yourself shine and "vibe high."

Dear Future Lover,

What is your vibration? I hope it's high. We will have such an amazing life together, because we are both high-vibe people.

I wonder what we'll accomplish in the world. Together, we'll be doing something. I haven't uncovered what that is yet, but it's there. I can feel it. We are destined to help people.

It's been a slow ride up for me. By the end of my marriage, I was very depressed (as is common for people who have been emotionally abused). But with lots of work, some really fantastic teachers, many great books, and an interest in feeling better, I've been able to raise my vibration. Sometimes I can even get it up to over 800 (that's out of 1000 according to David Hawkins, author of "Power vs. Force"). At this point, it's a game for me to see how high I can get it. And you know what? It's fun.

I hope you like to raise your vibration. Wait...I know you do.

Vibing high,

J

So, what actually happened?
How did this letter influence the outcome?

My vibration remains high most of the time. And my husband maintains a steady happiness. This is worth a lot.

CHAPTER 44

FEEL

What Feeling Are You Truly Going For?

Very often, when we ask for something, we can see it coming in only one or two ways. But the Universe doesn't work like this. You'll most often receive the "feeling essence" of what you ask for in unexpected ways.

When you're planning your desires, it's important to focus on the actual feeling you're trying to get when your dreams, hopes, wishes, and desires are fulfilled. After all, we do things because of the feelings they give us.

For example, say your desire is a new car. You'd like to have a fast car, maybe a Ferrari. You imagine yourself zipping down the highway with a big smile on your face. What is your primary purpose for getting this type of car? You may answer that it will help you get to work. Ah, but dig deeper.

Why is this a big deal? Perhaps you're always late and are looking for an edge to help you arrive on time. Or perhaps your idol has a Ferrari, and you always imagined that if you could be driving one too then you would be just like your idol.

Are you always late? You may be going for feeling that moment of "ahhh" when you leisurely walk through the doors at work with time to spare. In this case, the car could give you the "ahhh" feeling. If you focus on the feeling, things will start to line up in your life to give you the feeling…even if you never get the new car.

Would the car be a success symbol? Maybe you're going for a feeling that's a confirmation of your success. The proud "stick your chest out and show the world how well you're doing" feeling. If this is so, be careful as to what is underneath. Are you feeling inadequate? If that's what you are vibrating, then that's what you will get—more experiences that will match the inadequate feeling. Be sure you're vibrating the feelings you desire, and then treat them as if you already have them.

Need a stylish way to move from point A to point B? Perhaps you feel like you can step out a little bit, but you're still hiding behind the idea that a car is meant to move you between two locations. Will you feel embarrassed because others don't have your good fortune? Are you trying to justify the new Ferrari to others?

Each reason has an underlying feeling. It's up to you to decide what you're truly going after. Even if you don't know it, the Universe does, and it will deliver the feeling you're asking for.

This isn't as hard as it seems. Just keep digging until you uncover the feeling. Look for the actual physical sensation (not just the words) that you'll have when you feel that feeling. Then put your focus there and let go of how it shows up. Inevitably, it will turn up in many forms…with a new car being a possibility, but not the *only* way to get the feeling.

Often when you get to the underlying feelings, you'll feel something like an expansive feeling of space, a deep breath, relaxed shoulders, or your insides unwinding.

Listen to your body. Ask, "Body, what will I feel when I am in a relationship with my lover?" Then feel the sensations that appear in your body. The sensations are there to give you information…this may even be that you desire a different future. Or they could let you know that you're scared of this future and are building roadblocks to getting it. Or you feel expansive and excited about this future lover being in your life.

To clear that feeling (remember, it isn't the one you'll feel when you have your desire), ask yourself, "Am I willing to release and let go whatever this sensation is?" Answer the question. Answer, "Yes." However, if it's no, then ask yourself, "What is the advantage of holding onto this sensation?" Once you recognize the advantage, you'll have more information to help you feed the feeling.

Additional questions that will help are:

- ♥ What is the feeling trying to tell me?
- ♥ Am I willing to give up whatever I'm feeling right now?
- ♥ Am I willing to choose something different?
- ♥ If I could change this, what would I choose?
- ♥ Does it want to change?
- ♥ If I had unlimited possibilities, what would I choose right now?

Often, we think a feeling is permanent. "I'll never…" or "I'm always…." But there's no such thing as *never* and *always*. What? Remember the principle about truth? *It's only true until it's not.* You loved your first love until you didn't. You crawled until you walked.

Now, go back to your body and continue asking questions (especially clearing ones) until you're neutral about the desired feeling. If you take the time to identify the sensation you are striving for and then peel away what doesn't match, you can experience the feeling more and more. You can clear away the old feelings or you can step right into the new ones. It's your choice. Do you choose to get into the nitty-gritty of what you used to feel, or do you choose to be open to the possibility of what you *hope* to feel? In the end, it's a choice. Now at this point, you're ready to do things to help you feed the feeling.

Dear Future Lover,

Where were you this weekend? As things turned out, I had the days open. It's a rare treat to have the house to myself.

There are so many choices of things to do, but I chose to read romances—and not just any romances—Nora Roberts. They're usually filled with too much sex, but Shoshi assured me these weren't. Well—at least there was less. But, the end result was that you could have benefited from the reading. So, I repeat, where were you this weekend?

Obviously, you aren't the date who stood me up on Friday night. It was amazing that I wasn't bothered by it, which then bothered me on a different level. But while I waited at the restaurant, I enjoyed a glass of wine and read Quantum Enigma. I always carry a book with me, especially when I show up early.

Oh. Something funny—the man sitting next to me at the bar leaned over and asked what I was reading. When I showed him the cover, he said, "You can read that and drink at the same time?"

I found it very funny! I enjoyed the book, and my version of drinking is a half of a glass of wine over an hour. Now had it been water, I could have had a pitcher.

Waiting for you,

J

So, what actually happened?
How did this letter influence the outcome?

My husband supports my studies wholeheartedly. And as for benefiting from my reading romances, he's all for it.

CHAPTER 45

FEED THE FEELING

**Feed the Sensations You Will Have
When You Have Your Future**

What you focus on is what you get. Once you choose your desire, it's time to feed the feeling. The more you do to feed the feeling, the more you'll experience the actual sensation. Thus, your desire won't be the only way to experience the feeling.

Do things that will create the sensation you're aiming for. Take a walk. Exercise. Breathe deeply. Listen to music. Read a book that matches the feeling you desire. Go to the beach. Find things you're grateful for, and feel the gratitude. Ask lots of questions to create wiggle room for something to be different. Imagine your energy as being infinite…going all the way out to the stars and beyond. Do something fun, or just imagine you are doing something fun and feel it as if you were actually doing it. Laugh with friends.

A side note about those friends. Did you know that you become like the five people you most frequently hang out with? Who is feeding your feelings? Remember when your mom said, "Choose your friends wisely"? This is why.

Back to feeding your feelings…Sometimes you can shift the energy in a moment or two. Other times, it takes longer or you need to try multiple activities. Honor what you feel, but know that you can choose something that truly works for you. And from this place, you can choose something even better than that.

When you slip down the vibrational scale from the juicy feelings, know that it's not permanent. It's only true until it's not.

What you focus on is what you get—a simple principle that most people forget. We get so stuck (often in the negative, because people around us are complaining) that we forget that things can be different. However you feel and whatever you focus on is only a habit. You can choose to focus on what you *do* desire. Then it just takes a little practice, which is really just repetition.

If you're whining, moaning and groaning in the letters to your future lover, would that be attractive? Is your writing feeding the feeling you hope to have *when* you're in your relationship? Probably not. Instead, talk, act, and feel as if you are already with your lover and are excited to share what went on during the day. This is much more attractive. To attract a lover who is also positive and excited by what happens in life, you have to actually feel positive and excited about *your* life.

Pay attention to what you focus on. Is it what you hope to happen? Or is it what you hope *doesn't* happen? The Universe doesn't hear the word "not" and will give you what you *don't* want. Shift your focus to shift your life.

And here's an important point: The more you practice something, the better you get at it. What you practice becomes a habit. So, start doing things that will help you feel more expansive, move you closer and closer to high-vibe sensations, and create more ease in your life.

The more often you feed the feeling of your desire, the more you'll feel it, and the more you'll tell the Universe, "This is what I desire." From there, your dreams, hopes, wishes, and desires will start to appear because what shows up on the outside (life experiences) is just a reflection of what you feel on the inside.

Dear Future Lover,

The absence of your heartbeat made last night so long. I needed you beside me—reassuring, comforting, crawling inside my existence. Instead, I lay awake jittery with need until your pillow substituted for you, and I hugged it up against me as I imagined my arms around you, smelling your scent, feeling your heartbeat.

But alas, the beat was only the gentle vibration of the chi machine (a little triangular machine to help calm the central nervous system) nestled between my womb and the pillow. Though still enough to calm me down, I would have preferred you in the flesh.

When will this separation be over? When will we be together—if not again, then for the first time?

I thought these letters would bring us together, but I never anticipated the longing they would create. A longing different than before. There is more to be explored here.

Hugging you tightly,

J

So, what actually happened?
How did this letter influence the outcome?

Bruce is constantly saying that he decided to be happy no matter what. He chose a high-vibration feeling and feeds that feeling. He's even happy when watching all the political drama that plays out daily in Washington. He doesn't get stressed by much. This is something that certainly is a positive addition in my life.

CHAPTER 46

SILENCE

Take Time to Listen

One of the inspired actions you can always take is to do nothing…or more correctly, to be quiet. This inspired action merits its own section because it's so important, and it's often overlooked. Quiet, often accomplished through meditation, allows your inner thoughts to surface. If you pay attention to them, you'll be able to see if they match the desired feelings you now feed intentionally.

To be quiet, close your mouth and breath. *It's that simple.*

What do you focus on? Your breathing. Make every inhale and exhale a conscious slow breath. This will slow your heart rate and bring oxygen to the cells and more blood to the internal organs. It will even lower the adrenaline in your body. And as an added bonus, you will relax. Problems have trouble existing when you're relaxed.

This silence gives you the space to hear what the Universe is saying to you. And if you truly hope to have your future lover, it's worth opening up to see what the Universe has to say. This may be the whisper that leads you to your next tiny step on your path to your future lover.

Dear Future Lover,

The teens are so loud tonight. I love having their parties here, but sometimes they can get a bit loud. Adam doesn't even like to call his gatherings a party. According to him, he just "has people over." He can call it whatever he likes. To me, it's a party.

So, what am I doing writing now? I'm taking a break from walking the party. You see, the kids and all their friends know that if people are over, I'm nearby. The parties I love the most are the smaller ones where we all end up talking in the kitchen. This is when I really get to know the kids' friends. And I have to say, my kids have great friends.

Tomorrow will be a quiet day. We'll all be resting up from tonight. I wonder if I'll hear the remnants of the party in the quiet of tomorrow. It's an interesting thought.

That reminds me—Shoshi and Jen agree that, when they walk through the dining room, they can hear voices as if a party is going on even when the house is quiet. They've both experienced ghosts and such. I think this is cool, and I'm not afraid. Of course, it helps that I have the rule that everything benefits me.

So, what would benefit me right now? A little bit of quiet. Maybe I'll meditate for a few minutes before returning to walking the party.

I sure hope you like having kids over. Our house has been known to be party central at times.

Love,

J

So, what actually happened?
How did this letter influence the outcome?

Luckily, my husband is all right when we have lots of friends over. In fact, one time I was at a seminar in San Diego, and Adam asked if he could have a few friends over for his birthday. I said it was fine, as Shoshi and Bruce were both at home. What started out as a few friends blossomed into a social media nightmare.

That was the last (and only) birthday I missed. But he turned 23 this year, so I think we're safe. As for the quiet, Bruce and I both meditate now, although, it took a few years to get to this point.

Chapter 47

PLAY AND LAUGH

Play Is the Creative Energy

By being fully immersed in play and joy, you won't be distracted by concerns. Your thoughts will come together in new ways, and this allows you to make new connections. These new connections are the result of the creative spark—play.

Remember, you're creating your future lover. If you already had him, you wouldn't need to create him. To create your lover (or anything else), it helps to raise your vibration by playing, wondering, and asking "What else is possible?" After all, if you only look at what is and repeat that, then you aren't truly creating.

When you play and laugh, you don't worry about rules and structure. Rules, structure, and judgment seem to kill the creation process. Just have fun! Learn something new. Do something you love. Laugh with your friends. Do things that make you feel *great* (which by the way is a whole lot better than just feeling *good*). Once you're in the space of feeling great, ideas will pop up.

In my imagination, I think of God up in the sky with a salt shaker. He shakes crystals of ideas that fall to earth. Some people don't see them. Some pick up the crystals, look at them, and don't do anything. Others pick them up and wonder and play with them. The people in the last group *create*.

Personally, I was very serious and had to learn how to play. This is an ongoing challenge that is getting easier and easier. Recently, I invited friends over for my birthday. My intention for our time together was laughter…and we certainly did a lot of that. The laughter and fun allowed the pressure of the previous week to dissipate. When I came back to my writing, I wrote a chapter that my daughter said was my best work yet. And I've continued to create (for example, a really nice intimate moment with my husband). You get the idea. When you feel great, you create.

Dear Future Lover,

Jen, my friend, and I met for dinner tonight—Cheesecake Factory—loud—lots of talking. The first thing she said as we sat down was, "So tell me about him." When I looked confused, she said, "Oh, you haven't met him yet. He's caramel and there's nothing wrong."

She felt a strong wave of energy as she started to call me earlier in the evening. She was so excited about it, but she doesn't know what "caramel" means. Smooth? Sweet? Skin color? Smell? Somehow caramel is tied to this man.

I revealed what Jahner and I have been matrixing—relationships and fun. She said, "Whatever you're doing, keep doing it." It made me feel good.

You're just around the corner—the energetic corner, that is.

Jahner pointed out that I push away from fun, and I've never had a fun relationship, so subconsciously why would I want one? Good question. We cleared this and more for three hours.

Then for the next few days, all my resistance to fun came back, and I plunged into depression. Then, miraculously, it lifted as I talked with Anezka. Her intention for the matrix was to reveal the block to success. After a wild visual that had her smoking a peace pipe with an anvil, it came to me (in visual form) that she has one foot in the old energy, afraid to let go, and one foot in the new consciousness energy, afraid to trust the leap into it.

I joked about being right there with her. We certainly laughed a lot about the strange visualizations I was coming up with.

But the part about one foot in the old and one foot in the new resonated with me also. So, this morning when I awoke from a disturbing dream, I was determined to change the energy. Thus, the intention for today was to take one step toward the new energy—and I did. After walking Cole B and eating breakfast (soft boiled eggs and veggie stir fry), I sat down to read Dianetics. Jen's been after me to try it, as it's supposed to be even deeper than Release Technique. Since we were meeting for dinner, I quickly "read" the three Dianetics books I'd bought.

It started out as PhotoReading with mindmapping, a form of visual outlining. But by the second book, I was interested, so I continued mindmapping as a way to organize the information. I "read" and researched for about five hours. It occurred to me that my fun is researching. When Belinda and others told me to stop reading, I was lost and the fun left.

But now that I know, which is really just a reminder (as I already knew I liked research), I can do more. The difference this time is that mindmapping feels more free-form and less restrictive—the same reason I like Matrix Energetics.

If you're perfect for me, then you'll also be less restrictive. I wonder how this will show up. Job? Clothing? Hobby? Go-with-the-flow personality? I'm looking forward to finding out.

Loving you already,

J

So, what actually happened?
How did this letter influence the outcome?

Bruce has a totally different approach to fun. In fact, he's my "fun coach," and he's encouraging me to expand what I consider to be fun. We have gone to sprint car races, traveled around the world, and laughed together as we grabbed a quick kiss in the elevator. He even got me on a wave runner, and I love it! I wonder what the next fun adventure will be.

And as for the caramel? He's definitely sweet...and he likes caramel.

CHAPTER 48

INSPIRED ACTION

Prepare for the Arrival of Your Desires

Action is striking the match that starts the fire. Dreaming, visualizing, and feeling are the fuel, but the action is using the match. If you never do anything, there's nothing to bring it into reality. You can dream of meeting the future lover of your dreams, but if you never get out of your dreaming chair, it's a pretty good bet that he may have a hard time finding you. For example, he may be the plumber or electrician, but if you don't initiate the phone call or answer the door, you may not meet him. If you don't take actions then you are limiting the possibilities.

Your job is to prepare for the arrival of the desire (in this case, your future lover), knowing that it will come. This preparation could look like clearing out the cobwebs in your thinking, learning more about the desire, making decisions that will allow the desire to show up, learning everything you can about your desire, and feeling the chosen feelings as often as possible. In the case of inviting in your future lover, you may choose to clear out half of the garage for him, move over in bed and sleep on "your" side, and so on.

Taking action is about listening to your inner voice as it whispers to you what your next inspired action (next tiny step) could be. The key word here is "inspired." Somewhere along the way, an idea will pop up. It may be to go to the beach. It may be to reach for a certain book. It may be to go to an art gallery or restaurant. It may be to exercise in some way. It may be to write the next letter that's knocking on the door of your conscious mind. Whatever it is, honor your body. It's trying to lead you in the direction of your desire. It may not make sense at the moment, but the Universe has a plan to guide your desire to you. It's your job to follow the signs, which in this case are the actions you're inspired to do.

Traditional thinking is that you need to spend 90% of your efforts on work and 10% on inspiration. This is a low-vibe approach. The consciousness transformation approach is to spend the majority of your time on the inspiration, as well as imagining your desire and raising your vibration.

Follow the inspired action to the next tiny step. You don't have to know how or why it fits into the larger plan. You just make the choice and follow through by doing it. The idea is to manifest the steps and follow the feeling. Don't be limited by other people's ideas that "we have to do it their way." Follow the feeling to the next best step as it is ready to manifest.

For example, remember how I met my husband on a cruise? Well, if I had done things logically and according to other people's ideas, I wouldn't have gone on the cruise at all. It was during high school gymnastics season, and I was a volunteer assistant coach at the time. Logic would say that my responsibility was with the girls. But as the fourth coach—a volunteer at that—I took the plunge and went on the cruise. And because I took the inspired action (going on the cruise), I was a step closer to my desire (meeting my husband).

How did I know this was the "right" inspired action? It felt expansive. I listened to my body. When I asked, "Will this cruise expand my energy? In 50 years? In 100 years?" The expansiveness felt like my whole being was opening up. So, I took the next action and signed up for the cruise.

When you're open to all the possibilities, you don't have to do things in logical steps of one, two, and then three. You can do steps three, 20, 60, and *then* one. Or there may be no logic in the step at all. This is how inspired actions lead you to your desires... one step at a time. The difference is which steps we choose to do as a high-vibrational being. The person with creative vision will see the steps, but in a different form. She doesn't care what the steps are; she just knows that they'll lead to the end result.

Dear Future Lover,

It seems as if I'm writing you at least once a week at this point. Well, this past week, I had some interesting insights.

First, when athletes visualize something before doing it, I always understood the value, but the mechanics were fuzzy. Then this week, I was watching a TED Talk, and while I was watching, the thought "camera angles" came to mind. When I visualize something, it's as if the camera angle is looking at the event. However, if I change the angle from looking at the event to looking out of my own eyes as I "do it" then the whole experience changes. It was a real eye-opener!

Second, I was flipping channels in the middle of the night and came across a channel with soft porn. (I don't know how they get away with it, but they do). As I flipped past it, I saw one of the "ladies." She was muscular—not soft at all. Again, a thought flitted through my head. It never occurred to me that a woman can be muscular and sexy. It was like a light bulb going off—another layer of my ex's rejections was peeled away. Wow!

> Third, another TED Talk speaker said that it was worthwhile to spread joy. I laughed as my mind went to my spreading (expanding) hips. Spreading joy. Do you get it?
>
> Laughing,
>
> J

So, what actually happened?
How did this letter influence the outcome?

We both used inspired actions to go on the cruise and meet each other. In addition, Bruce uses inspired actions when he creates his inventions and comes up with new ideas. And some of these ideas have been a "very creative" and even funny.

For example, he knows that people feel better after having an MRI, so he decided to experiment with magnets and brain clarity by putting some very strong magnets on a metal helmet. I have to say, he looked very funny with this magnetized helmet on his head as he watched TV. In following the inspired actions, he is kick starting his brain.

(I wouldn't recommend making this helmet for yourself. The placement of the magnets is crucial and can cause problems if they are not placed correctly.)

CHAPTER 49

ACT "AS IF"

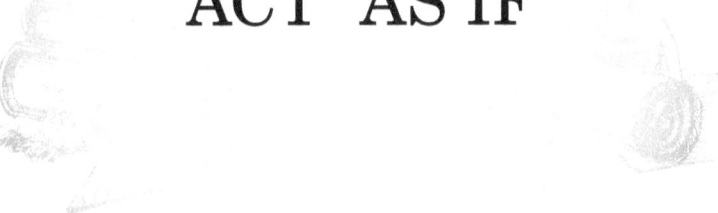

Pretend You Already Have Your Lover

Pulling the future into the now is important. Feel as if you already have it. Why?

Because it changes the energy from *yearning* and *wanting* to actually *having*. It changes the feeling in your body.

It's actually very simple. Pretend you already have your lover. If you did, what would you do, say, or feel? Now do, say, and feel it...even if it doesn't make sense. You're sleeping in the middle of a big bed? Move over and give your lover some room. You eat standing up at the sink? Set the table (including a spot for your lover) and carry on a conversation with him. You run out of the house in a hurry? Imagine kissing your lover goodbye on your way out, and feel what that feels like...every time you leave. You get the idea.

Imagine yourself sending cards to your lover. You can stop there and know it's something you will do in the future, but this keeps it in the future. *Or* you can act as if your lover is already in your life, and go out and actually buy cards! By taking this action, you're showing the Universe that you're serious about your desire and are, in fact, preparing for it. And since your focus is on actually having the lover (versus just yearning for one), the Universe will line things up so this can happen.

In addition, give gratitude for already having your desire. This is what prayer is meant to be...giving thanks in advance. Assume it's already done. By giving thanks and feeling gratitude, your vibration will rise. Since gratitude is a high vibration, things will happen with more ease in your life...including your lover showing up.

It doesn't have to cost a lot of money. But it does take some initiative to act "as if."

Dear Future Lover,

Laughter, melting into the floor, hallucinating out of our friggin' minds—these are all the norm at a Matrix Energetics seminar. I'm having so much fun and also learning a lot. The science is a little over my head, but I'm getting the gist of it.

Some of the techniques Richard, the teacher, is teaching are familiar. I do them from Yuen, Spring Forest Qigong, or even Release Technique. I sure hope you're connected to Matrix or are at least willing to be. It's a riot.

Tonight, I asked Wendy (from South Africa) about what to do with my hair. She said that earlier in the evening, she actually saw me with shorter hair. Then, as we stood in the hotel lobby, she matrixed my hair. Peter (from Maine) couldn't stand up. Every time he tried, he fell to the floor again. We were all laughing. "A man at my feet. Bless you my child." Even Esther (from Colorado) was laughing. Then Wendy asked if I wanted her to cut my hair. It was close. I almost said yes. So, we matrixed the style Wendy was seeing to my hairdresser. I wonder how it's going to turn out.

What a great way to live—letting go of my attachments to a specific outcome. That's what makes Matrix so effective. It truly takes advantage of all the possibilities. I wish I remembered to use it more often. I'll just matrix that. Poof. Drool. Splat. Settle. There it is. Insert.

Intention—matrix—I wonder. You have to give this a try. I'll just matrix you to the Matrix experience. Did you feel it? It's that easy. Enjoy.

Love,

J

Note: The letters are not in the order I wrote them. As in this letter, I'm still thinking about cutting my hair and in a previous letter in an earlier chapter, I had done it already.

So, what actually happened?
How did this letter influence the outcome?

Actually, there are times that I forget to matrix a situation and Bruce reminds me to do it. Other times, I'm reminding him. We have each other's backs.

CHAPTER 50

REM

Repetition. Emotion. Motion.

Let's say you have the wording for your desire exactly how you like it. How do you magnetize your desire? Increase the intensity of the feeling. Feel it more often and deeply. The more you focus on the feeling, the more the feeling will be in your body.

This shows up as repetition, emotion, and motion—"REM." Feel it over and over through various activities (repetition). Increase the intensity of the feeling you're striving for (emotion). And finally, add movement to the feeling (motion).

This is the "practice" part. Repetition, emotion, and motion are how you practice. If you know that your desire is to feel loved, start by feeling love for yourself, over and over. Next, do things that will help you love yourself more intensely, such as writing yourself a love letter or standing in front of the mirror and noticing all the things you love about yourself. Then, add a motion such as stroking your forearm as a lover would.

The more you do it, the more you feel it and the more your desire will be magnetized to you. Writing letters to your future lover is one example of how to use REM. There are many letters; you have written with emotion; and you've taken the action of writing or typing.

Once you include REM, your dreams will be brought forth.

> Dear Reader,
>
> Every letter applies here.
>
> Love,
>
> J

So, what actually happened?
How did this letter influence the outcome?

I found a great guy and we're married…even though when we first met, Bruce said he was never getting married again, and I said I was. I kept practicing REM and expanding into the space where I knew we would be married.

I kept my eye on the dream and followed the inspired actions I was led to do. We'd been looking at rings (his inspired action). Then I said, "But, you haven't asked me yet." A few weeks went by and then one night as I was falling asleep he leaned over and whispered, "Will you marry me?" I flipped over. Said, "Yes." Kissed him. And then rolled over and went to sleep. We joke that he was trying to sneak it in hoping that I'd already fallen asleep. And then he could say he asked, even if I didn't hear it.

My focusing on the dream through REM helped bring it into reality.

CHAPTER 51

NOW

The Only Time Is This Moment

You have only this moment. That's right—the only thing that exists is *now*. The past is just a series of now moments that have already taken place. The future is a series of now moments that have yet to happen. All you have is this now moment.

If you choose to, you can waste your now moment worried about the past or fearful about the future. But a different choice may be to put your all into the moment you are experiencing *right now*.

And if you're imagining your future lover, bring him into this now moment. Make him as real as if he already exists, for he does. He's out there somewhere…as well as being a creation in your mind. So, get busy and start creating, so he can show up. *It's your time now.*

In this moment, start dreaming. Play with your thoughts and see what shows up. Choose the high vibe you desire. Say to yourself, "In this moment, I choose to be _____." Fill in the blank with your desired high vibe. Pretend you are talking with your best friend and you are really expounding on this. Put as many details into it as you can. This is a dream phase. Choose the high vibe you would like to be. Then start doing things to expand that sensation.

Continue dreaming. Choose the feeling you will feel (the actual physical sensations) *when* you are in the relationship. Again, start with, "In this moment, I choose _____." The more you can identify and dream about the feelings, the more they can become a reality.

Next, dream about your intention for the relationship. If it were perfect, what would you choose it to be? Let your imagination run wild. This whole process is fun if you allow yourself to be creative.

Since you are bringing your future lover into the now, you are ready to write. If you were to write to him right now, what might you say? Be open to what shows up.

If you haven't already begun, start your journal now. And anywhere that you are blocking yourself from writing to your future lover, are you willing to release and let it go forever? Yes? Good. Now, begin with this:

Dear Future Lover,

Appendix A

PROMPTS

Questions You Can Ask Yourself

These questions are focused mostly on you. Just turn them around to ask your future lover about his ideas. Simply change the "I" to "you" to ask your future lover the questions. If it's too frightening to think of an actual lover for yourself, perhaps you can ease into it by thinking of these questions as if they refer to your book boyfriend.

After you ask the questions, an "answer" will pop up in your awareness. If nothing does or if you are feeling a sensation (such as a tightening in your chest or throat) then use the opportunity to clear the sensation. Ask yourself, "Whatever that is about, am I willing to release and let it go forever?" You may have to ask a few times, but the sensation will change and an answer will appear.

I wish I had thought of these questions when I wrote my journal. It would have been even more focused and useful. Do not feel you have to answer all of the following questions—skim them. Whatever questions stand out or thoughts pop up are the ones you pay attention to.

When you think of other questions, GREAT! Follow those, as long as they feel expansive.

- ♥ What am I willing to do to raise my vibration?
- ♥ What vibration would I like to be at most of the time?
- ♥ What would it take for me to raise my vibration just a little bit?
- ♥ What can I be or do right now to raise my vibration or energy?
- ♥ What can I be or do right now to feel even better?
- ♥ What is the highest vibration I'm willing to be? What am I willing to do to get there?
- ♥ What qualities am I looking for in my future lover?
- ♥ If someone walked into my life today with these qualities, what would I feel?
- ♥ What would it feel like to have this person in my life?
- ♥ What will it take to recognize someone with these qualities and feelings?
- ♥ What actions will he do that demonstrate them?
- ♥ What would it take for me to feel the love for my future self? (Pretend he's in front of you and you have the feeling already.)
- ♥ What is happening in my everyday life that is showing up differently from what I imagined?
- ♥ What expectations do I have that are attracting what is showing up?
- ♥ What do I imagine my relationship with my future lover will feel like once it arrives?
- ♥ What feelings surprise me?
- ♥ What are the feelings I hope to feel when I'm with my future lover?
- ♥ What am I willing to let go of so I can have the feelings I desire?
- ♥ What phrases am I repeating (to myself or out loud) that are unfounded assumptions?

- ♥ What am I holding onto that is only an assumption? Do I need to hold onto it or can I let it go?
- ♥ What assumptions would I like to make?
- ♥ What is getting in the way of those assumptions coming true?
- ♥ If I could choose any assumption in the world, what might that be?
- ♥ What am I waffling on that if I weren't, I could make a decision?
- ♥ What can I share about myself to show the real me?
- ♥ If I could be vulnerable right now, what would I share?
- ♥ What are my thoughts about being vulnerable in a relationship?
- ♥ What type of vulnerability am I looking for from my future lover?
- ♥ What is the feeling I'm feeling right now?
- ♥ Is this the feeling I hope to convey to my future lover?
- ♥ If I wanted to convey a different feeling, what would that be?
- ♥ What gets me excited?
- ♥ What makes me tick?
- ♥ What am I afraid of?
- ♥ What does truth feel like to me?
- ♥ What am I accepting as truth, but haven't yet asked my body if it is, in fact, truth?
- ♥ What lies am I telling myself?
- ♥ What am I hoping is truth, but deep down realize that something is off?
- ♥ What would it take to listen to my body and what it truly desires?
- ♥ What opinions about my future am I holding onto?

- ♥ What am I resisting that if I weren't resisting I could make a choice and move on?
- ♥ What about my past relationships am I bringing into this relationship that if I let go of I could have an amazing relationship—better than anything I could ever have imagined?
- ♥ What am I not at peace about?
- ♥ What helps me feel at peace?
- ♥ What signs am I asking for?
- ♥ What signs am I not noticing that if I were to broaden my awareness I would notice?
- ♥ What am I asking for signs about?
- ♥ What are the signs prompting me to do or not do?
- ♥ What is happening around me that is teaching me something or highlighting an "aha moment"?
- ♥ What would it take to be my most expansive self?
- ♥ If my life or future relationship were filled with peace and calm, gratitude and kindness, what would show up?
- ♥ What does my future life/relationship look like?
- ♥ What gift am I ready to accept?
- ♥ If I imagine my future lover, what gifts will he bring to the relationship?
- ♥ What am I taking responsibility for in my life?
- ♥ What could I take responsibility for?
- ♥ What am I taking responsibility for in my sex life?
- ♥ If I were truly intimate, what would that look and feel like?
- ♥ What am I blaming others for, that if I let go of the blame, I could stop being a victim?
- ♥ What circumstances in my life still pop up as something I complain about?
- ♥ What would I like to forgive someone else for?
- ♥ What would I like to forgive myself for?

- ♥ Have I ever forgiven someone in the past? What did that feel like?
- ♥ If I'm holding onto a resentment, am I willing to let it go forever, never to bother me again?
- ♥ What am I holding onto about past relationships that if I forgave them (or myself) I would be able to come to this relationship free of anything from the past?
- ♥ If I were to pretend that my lover was in front of me right now, what would I do?
- ♥ When I look at my lover, what do I see? What is my reaction?
- ♥ What could I shift in my living space to allow my lover to have room?
- ♥ Am I willing to kiss my lover right now?
- ♥ If I could buy something for my lover, what might that be?
- ♥ What do I like to do when I play?
- ♥ When I play, what does it feel like?
- ♥ If there were no barrier to playing, what would I like to do?
- ♥ When in my past have I played and had an idea pop up in my mind?
- ♥ What are my subconscious thoughts about playing?
- ♥ What decision am I waiting to make that, if I made it, I could say YES! with joy?
- ♥ If I were to write my eulogy, what might it say?
- ♥ What are my feelings about my future relationship?
- ♥ What would it take for me to say YES with joy! to this relationship?
- ♥ If I were to put one foot forward, where or what would I step toward?
- ♥ What acknowledgments can I give myself?

- ♥ What acknowledgments can I give my future lover?
- ♥ What is happening in my life that I'd like to share with my future lover?
- ♥ Where am I coherent within my life?
- ♥ What have I done today to bring my thoughts, feelings, and actions into coherence?
- ♥ If I had flow in my life, where would it show up?
- ♥ What am I willing to be, have, and do to create my future lover?
- ♥ What am I not willing to allow and accept that, if I were willing to allow and accept, I would feel more at ease?
- ♥ If I looked at something that just happened, what could I allow that I hadn't allowed before?
- ♥ What is blocking my allowance and acceptance?
- ♥ What am I willing to allow and accept from my future lover?
- ♥ What am I unwilling to allow and accept from my future lover?
- ♥ If I imagine the final scene of the movie in which my future lover and I are the stars, what do I picture?
- ♥ If I were the movie director, what would the viewer see and feel?
- ♥ What am I sensing? (Use all your senses.)
- ♥ If it could be even better than that, what would it be?
- ♥ What relationships do I see that I never noticed before?
- ♥ What relationship do I have with myself?
- ♥ What relationship do I have with my future lover?
- ♥ What is my future lover's relationship to me?
- ♥ What relationship does my connection with my future lover have to the world?

- ♥ What is my relationship with my journal letters to my future lover?
- ♥ What is the journal's relationship to me?
- ♥ What is around me that I've never "seen" before but has been there?
- ♥ What is so important about holding onto my point of view and not seeing something else?
- ♥ What judgments are limiting what I see?
- ♥ What is the benefit of seeing something new about my future lover?
- ♥ If I were to observe my future lover, what would I see?
- ♥ What do I imagine my relationship with my future lover will feel like once it arrives?
- ♥ What feelings surprise me?
- ♥ What feelings do I hope to feel when I'm with my future lover?
- ♥ What am I imagining about my future that I could start feeling right now?
- ♥ What can I focus on to feed the feeling of how I desire to feel?
- ♥ If I could feel "that" right now, what would that feel and look like?
- ♥ What are the sensations I'll experience when I have that feeling?
- ♥ What feelings will my future lover have when we meet?
- ♥ What feelings will my future lover have when we're together? Apart?
- ♥ What feelings do I have when I'm with this person? Apart from this person?
- ♥ What am I aware of now that I wasn't aware of yesterday?

- ♥ What must I perceive and know about the relationship to bring it into reality?
- ♥ What must I perceive and know about myself to raise my vibration?
- ♥ What do I choose to be aware of *now* about my future lover?
- ♥ What is my awareness about my true intention in desiring this new relationship?
- ♥ What did I do today to feed the feeling?
- ♥ What am I imagining about my future that I could start feeling right now?
- ♥ What can I focus on to feed the feeling of how I desire to feel?
- ♥ What could I do repeatedly to support my dream of a future lover?
- ♥ What would it take to feel my chosen feelings even more intensely?
- ♥ If I was to write about a motion that I imagine my future lover will do with me, what might that be?
- ♥ What future motion will I do with my lover?
- ♥ What would it take to do that future motion now?
- ♥ What is my habit in relationships?
- ♥ What habit do I have that limits how I show up in a relationship?
- ♥ Where am I limiting myself, that if I weren't, I could have everything I imagine?
- ♥ What are my friends saying that can contribute to my journal letters?
- ♥ What time limit am I using on things that, if I let go of, something different could happen?

- ♥ What idea keeps popping into my head that I've been ignoring? Is this an inspired action waiting for me to act on?
- ♥ If I knew my desire, what would it take to visualize and feel it?
- ♥ What is my heart leading me to do now?
- ♥ What have I run across that sparked an idea? What does that idea inspire me to do?
- ♥ If I were to take an inspired action now, what might it be?
- ♥ What have I done in my life that made no sense until after it was done and then the relevance was revealed?
- ♥ What would it take for me to hear the whispers of the Universe?
- ♥ When was the last time I was quiet with nothing going on except my breathing?
- ♥ What do I do to be quiet?
- ♥ What meditation practice do I follow?
- ♥ When do I like to meditate?
- ♥ What is perfect that I didn't see as perfect before?
- ♥ What is perfect about the time leading up to meeting my future lover?
- ♥ What growth have I had in my life since I started my *Dear Future Lover* letters?
- ♥ What is so vital about not meeting my future lover that it is keeping me stuck?
- ♥ What am I hungering for?

APPENDIX B

SUGGESTED READING

Books that will help you expand your thinking and further explain the principles presented in *Dear Future Lover*.

10% Happier, Dan Harris

As a Man Thinketh, James Allen

Being You, Changing the World, Dr. Dain Heer

Dare, Dream, Do, Whitney Johnson

Do You Quantum Think?, Dianne Collins

Hot Chocolate Happiness, Jeoffrey R. Hutcherson

It Works, RHJ

Life Visioning, Michael Bernard Beckwith

Love Yourself, Lawrence Crane

Personal Power through Awareness, Sanaya Roman

Power vs. Force, David R. Hawkins, M.D., PH. D

Quantum Leap Thinking, James J. Mapes

Staying Well with Guided Imagery, Belleruth Naparstek

The Biology of Belief, Bruce H. Lipton, PH. D

The Future is Yours, Raymon Grace

The Magic of Believing, Claude M. Bristol

The Magic of Thinking Big, David J. Schwartz, PH. D

The Magic Path of Intuition, Florence Scovel Shinn

The Physics of Miracles, Richard Bartlett, DC, ND

The Power of Awareness, Neville Goddard

The Power of Habit, Charles Duhigg

The Power of Your Subconscious Mind, Joseph Murphy, PH. D, D.D.

The Prosperity Secret, Markus Rothkranz

The Sacred Art of Lovingkindness, Rabbi Rami Shapiro

The Spontaneous Fulfillment of Desire, Deepak Chopra

The Ten Keys to Total Freedom, Gary M. Douglas & Dr. Dain Heer

The True Power of Water, Masaru Emoto

Think & Grow Rich, Napoleon Hill

Think or Sink, Gina Mollicone-Long

Yes! Energy, Loral Langemeier

You are a Badass, Jen Sincero

APPENDIX C

PRINCIPLES

Intention: Know what you're going for.

Expectations: You get what you expect.

Assumptions: Assumptions limit possibilities.

Decision Making: When you've made the decision, it's "done."

Feeling the Sensations: Identify the feeling you're truly after.

Release and Let it Go … Forever: Let go to have freedom.

Willingness: Willingness is the magic pill of change.

Wonder and Curiosity: The gateway to magic is in the sense of mystery.

Questions: The wiggle room is in the question.

Choice: The choice is yours.

Timing: It will show up when it shows up.

Possibilities: Keep reaching for a more useful possibility.

Rules: Beliefs we tell ourselves are true for us.

Perspective: Perspective determines reality.

Vibrations: Highest vibe wins.

Vibrational Match: Whatever you're feeling is what you're attracting.

High Vibes: Ease is found at love, peace, and gratitude.

Follow Through: Take the next tiny step.

Reach for a More Useful Feeling: Things can be even better.

Judgment: Let go of fixed points of view ... including judgments.

Be You: Quit compromising against yourself.

Feel the Truth: It's only true until it's not.

Neutrality: The art of being at peace.

Signs: Pay attention to the signs around you.

Infinite Beingness: Expand and be all of you.

Personal Responsibility: It's your life. Take responsibility for it.

Forgiveness: Forgive yourself and others.

Habits: Create new habits.

Perfection: What shows up is perfect ... on some level.

Create Your Future: You create your life.

YES!: Take charge of your life. Say YES!

Coherence: Flow with the river.

Awareness: There is nothing you need to be or do to be who you are.

Imagine: All of life is made up. Imagine your future.

Relationship: Balance the relationship to neutrality.

Acceptance and Allowance: "Should-bust" your way to a higher vibration.

Observe: Zip it, watch, and listen.

The Energy You *Be* is Vital: Be to become.

Boost Your Vibration: Be the true you.

Feel: What feeling are you truly going for?

Feed the Feeling: Feel the sensations you will have *when* you have your future.

Silence: Take time to listen.

Play and Laugh: Play is the creative energy.

Inspired Action: Prepare for the arrival of your desires.

Act "As If": Pretend you already have your lover.

REM: Repetition. Emotion. Motion.

Now: The only time is this moment.

ACKNOWLEDGMENTS

Thank You, Thank You, Thank You

A great big thank you goes to the following people for everything they did to help bring *Dear Future Lover* to fruition:

- ♥ **Kate Megregian:** Thank you for being my right-hand woman.
- ♥ **Sara Lubezny:** Thank you for getting this book ready for publication.
- ♥ **Dr. Ron Jahner:** Thank you for teaching me for the past 18 plus years. And thank you for believing in me when I didn't believe in myself.
- ♥ **Belinda Womack:** Thank you for all the support and lessons that you have provided throughout the past 17 years.
- ♥ **My children (Bethany, JT, Shoshanna and Adam):** Thank you for being you and coming along on this journey with me.
- ♥ **Teachers and Innovators:** A great big thank you to those of you who have come before me in this wonderful adventure of our made-up world. Dr. Richard Bartlett (Matrix Energetics), Dain Heer and Gary Douglas (Access Consciousness), Dr. Leonard Coldwell (Instinct Based Medicine System), Larry Crane and Lester Levinson (Release Technique), and Chunyi Lin (Spring Forest Qi Gong), Dr. Hector Garcia (Garcia Innergetics), and anyone else that has contributed to this field.

♥ **Inspiring Authors:** Thank you to all of the authors who have written books that have helped me learn about the principles and how consciousness transformation, energy healing, and the Law of Attraction actually work.

 And thanks to my Hubby for helping to make my dreams come true.

ABOUT THE AUTHOR

Judith Joy began studying energy healing and consciousness transformation because of recurring headaches. During her 20 years of research, she became fascinated with how the heart and mind work together to create this experience we call life. Her interest developed into a passion to transform lives into something truly magical and effervescent. Judith distills esoteric ideas into easy-to-understand concepts. She implements tools and techniques that she is excited to share with you so that you can be the best you and live a phenomenal life.

Judith is a dream creation coach, Matrix Energetics-certified practitioner, teacher, author, speaker, wife, mother, and grandmother. She is the author of *Surviving Your Teenager. . . and being happy anyway.* Using results from her own quest of self-discovery and study of energy and consciousness transformation systems, Judith helps people give an emphatic YES! to life with joy.

Find Judith at: www.judithjoy.com

www.ingramcontent.com/pod-product-compliance
Lightning Source LLC
Chambersburg PA
CBHW022215090526
44584CB00012BB/561